Student-Designed Games

Strategies for Promoting Creativity, Cooperation, and Skill Development

Peter Hastie, PhD

Auburn University

Library of Congress Cataloging-in-Publication Data

Hastie, Peter A., 1959-
  Student-designed games : strategies for promoting creativity, cooperation, and skill
development / Peter Hastie.
     p. cm.
  Includes bibliographical references and index.
  ISBN-13: 978-0-7360-8590-8 (soft cover)
  ISBN-10: 0-7360-8590-4 (soft cover)
  1. Educational games--Design and construction. 2. Simulation games in education--Design and construc-
tion. I. Title.
  LB1029.G3H37 2010
  371.39'7--dc22
                                  2010004508

ISBN-10: 0-7360-8590-4 (print)
ISBN-13: 978-0-7360-8590-8 (print)

The Web addresses cited in this text were current as of January 2010, unless otherwise noted.

Acquisitions Editor: Scott Wikgren; **Developmental Editor:** Jacqueline Eaton Blakley; **Assistant Editors:** Elizabeth Evans and Anne Rumery; **Copyeditor:** Patricia MacDonald; **Indexer:** Sharon Duffy; **Permission Manager:** Dalene Reeder; **Graphic Designer:** Bob Reuther; **Graphic Artist:** Tara Welsch; **Cover Designer:** Keith Blomberg; **Photographer (front and back covers):** Photos courtesy of Peter Hastie; **Photographer (interior):** Photos courtesy of Peter Hastie, unless otherwise noted; **Photo Production Manager:** Jason Allen; **Art Manager:** Kelly Hendren; **Associate Art Manager:** Alan L. Wilborn; **Illustrator:** Tammy Page; **Printer:** Versa Press

Printed in the United States of America   10 9 8 7 6 5 4 3 2 1

The paper in this book is certified under a sustainable forestry program.

Human Kinetics
Web site: www.HumanKinetics.com

United States: Human Kinetics
P.O. Box 5076
Champaign, IL 61825-5076
800-747-4457
e-mail: humank@hkusa.com

Canada: Human Kinetics
475 Devonshire Road Unit 100
Windsor, ON N8Y 2L5
800-465-7301 (in Canada only)
e-mail: info@hkcanada.com

Europe: Human Kinetics
107 Bradford Road
Stanningley
Leeds LS28 6AT, United Kingdom
+44 (0) 113 255 5665
e-mail: hk@hkeurope.com

Australia: Human Kinetics
57A Price Avenue
Lower Mitcham, South Australia 5062
08 8372 0999
e-mail: info@hkaustralia.com

New Zealand: Human Kinetics
P.O. Box 80
Torrens Park, South Australia 5062
0800 222 062
e-mail: info@hknewzealand.com

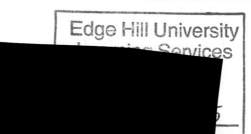

E4902

Contents

PART II   Designing Basic Games   43

Preface

Playing games is still considered by many as the most fun of all the areas of physical education. But too often, game play has been taught in physical education in ways that alienate or exclude many students (particularly girls and those with lower skill level). In *student-designed games*, all students are included; are free to explore methods of scoring; have their choice of equipment, space, and rules; and are limited only by their (and their teacher's) imaginations and the resources that are available. Consequently it has been suggested that games making provides opportunities for pupils to make and create a game that is theirs, discover why rules are important, work cooperatively and share their ideas, talk about game development, and teach others, including the teacher.

This book is written for preservice teachers and teachers at all levels of physical education instruction who wish to include student-designed games in their curriculum. In games-making units, students design their own games within certain limits presented by the teacher. At the most basic level, students can work with games they already play and manipulate the number of players on a side, the size of the court or field, the implements or balls used, or some simple rules. At higher levels of complexity, students can design games that are completely unique and present tactical problems not seen in any of the sports they historically play. Constantly changing materials (e.g., hockey sticks, tennis rackets), balls (e.g., softball, football, or balloon), and parts of the body used (hand, foot, head, or racket) serves to enhance students' motivation and creativity, and it has been noted that quite often these kinds of games elicit more interest than do teacher-designed games. As a result, teachers can use games making from as early as third grade up to and including university physical education courses.

This book meets a need in that current educational thought is focusing on more constructivist ways to stimulate students' learning, as well as the recent motivational literature that emphasizes the benefits of high-autonomy instructional climates. Where students are given choices and voice in their curriculum, motivation to participate is shown to increase significantly.

As noted, this book has content applicable for implementation for students at elementary through college levels. This allows teachers at all levels of schooling to take the key principles of games making and apply them within their physical education classes. The basic forms of games that constitute them remain consistent. All that changes is the sophistication of the rules that limit what players can and cannot do. Students at all grade levels, including college, are capable of either changing rules or creating new ones to make games that are exciting and fun to play. The material in part II that outlines the essential skill and tactical concepts of games can be used by teachers at all levels.

The book is organized into three parts. Part I first provides a background of games making and gives the reader key points as to the educational and motivational benefits that are derived when students create their own new games. This section also provides a clear outline of how to present lessons on games making and identifies the key instructional issues involved in lessons. Part II describes the five different categories in which we can place various games. The chapters first list the skills and concepts that are central to those games, and this is followed by sample games. Once the reader has a solid understanding of how these games work, each chapter has a template of questions that help stimulate students to begin designing their own games. Part III allows the reader to really extend the games-making process to create games that cross the more familiar game forms. A chapter is included on designing games that focus not on defeating an opponent but on challenging players to work with partners to achieve a particular performance target. The final chapter identifies ways in which students and teachers can evaluate games, particularly in terms of their utility and excitement.

Albert Einstein once wrote, "Imagination is more important than knowledge. Knowledge is limited. Imagination encircles the world." While understanding the value of imagination, and particularly its place in games making, any teacher will understand that although we may not need to be taught to play, we do need to be taught how to think in new ways. This book is designed to help teachers work with their students to develop tactical creativity. By creativity, we mean the ideas of originality and flexibility. Originality refers to the ideas of unusualness, innovativeness, rareness, or even uniqueness, while flexibility relates to the ease with which someone can use different systems of reference or modify information. The key feature of the book that helps is the game templates that are provided with each game form. Students can begin creating their games with simple questions so that they have some product with which to experiment. The chapter sections on key concepts and skills should help provide teachers with enough conceptual knowledge to then allow them to ask stimulus questions of their students as games are developed.

Acknowledgments

This book is dedicated to Dr. Ashley Casey (University of Bedfordshire) and the boys from 4B and 5B at Ripon Grammar School, North Yorkshire, UK. Their work in games making has helped take this book far beyond the scope it would have had without their contributions.

4B

Marcus Fenlon
Alex Gath-Walker
Chris Ogden
Andrew (Barry) Harrison
Lewis Haggerty
Fraser Birtwistle
George Lamb
Patrick Skelton
Alex Ellerby
Andrew Everett
Will Forbes
Harry Green
Ellis Hall
Ben Constable
Chris Wallace

5B

Oliver Jackson
Anthony Johnson
Peter Hogan
Theo Mortimer
Connor Culver
David James
Chris Mahoney
Ashley Lowe
Lewis Fletcher
Jay Mitchell
Andy Lincoln

I would also like to thank the following people who gave freely of their time and ideas:

- Anne-Marie Tarter, Ripon Grammar School
- Matt Curtner-Smith and Oleg Sinelnikov, University of Alabama
- Todd Layne, Auburn University
- Chuck Cooper and Corey Ivatt, Cary Woods School
- Amanda Brown, Tyler Daffon, Brent Greer, Ian Knapp, LaDextric Oliver, Davis Stephenson, Wesley Taff, Blake Wilkes, and Alison Link, Auburn University

Thanks also to all those at Human Kinetics who adopted the challenge to make this text the best it could be: Scott Wikgren, Jacqueline Blakley, Elizabeth Evans, Anne Rumery, Bob Reuther, Tara Welsch, and so many others involved with this project—their efforts have been outstanding.

I would also like to thank those who posed for and contributed to the photographs and artwork for this book.

Getting Started

- Understand how games making works.
- Learn how students benefit from designing games.
- Set the stage for success with effective teaching strategies.

If we consider this book to be a three-course meal, part I represents the appetizer. Here we set the table by describing the process of student-designed games and the type of class environment needed to make it successful (chapter 1). Games making, however, is no simple or frivolous diversion from more serious physical education endeavors. Part I also describes the educational benefits of student-designed games (chapter 2), as well as provides key strategies for teaching (chapter 3).

Part I continues by describing the various ways in which we can categorize games and how games can be grouped according to common tactical features (chapter 4). Examples of the five different major categories of games are given to help you enjoy the main course that follows: part II.

CHAPTER 1

An Introduction to Student-Designed Games

For many of us, some of our best childhood memories revolve around playing games after school with our friends. Most of the time, these games were created with whatever equipment we could muster (or make), and in all cases, they were free from adult interference. The games were formal in that they involved rules, teammates, and scores, but they were informal in that they were made by us, and for us, with the key goal of challenging our abilities in the name of fun. This spontaneity and creativity is so often missing in physical education, with the result that game play becomes the province of the most skillful to the exclusion of many others.

It is the purpose of this book to introduce you to the process of teaching games making as a way of engaging *all* students in your classes, essentially by *making* games for learning instead of *playing* games for learning.

By definition, games making in physical education is a process where students create, organize, implement, practice, and refine their own games within certain limits presented by the teacher. These games are considered a major tool for enhancing student interest, and some have suggested they often bring forth more interest than do teacher-designed games (Rovegno & Bandhauer, 1994).

Games making, is not, however, a simple case of the teacher giving students some equipment and saying, "Go make up a game." Taught well, games making provides a means through which students can do the following:

- Engage actively with and explore components of game play (skills and strategy) and, in turn, construct a deeper understanding of these components
- Think critically about their experiences playing games and sports at recess and after school
- Learn how to learn cooperatively and solve problems in groups

Games making involves a cycle of experimentation and refinement.

The key is that students follow a sequence of (1) design, (2) trial, and (3) refine to get to a point where the game is ready to be presented, explained, and demonstrated to the class before being played and evaluated by others.

A Brief Theory of Student-Designed Games

The fundamental premise underlying why students should be involved in game design is this: When anything is created, be it a piece of art, a delicious dessert, or a science project, the greatest learning benefit remains reserved for those engaged in the design process (the game designers), and not those at the receiving end. So it is with games. When we play traditional games, the game player is not part of the discussions involved in developing the ideas, designs, and strategies of those games.

Of further importance is that games making is a collaborative process. In designing games, student learning takes place within a culture in which there are rich interactions between members of the community (in our case, the class). These interactions are central to games making because groups not only work together to design games but also, by presenting and trialing them with other students, get feedback before the final product is presented. The games developed during units of student-designed games therefore become what are called shareable artifacts. These artifacts are *public entities* in that they are specifically designed to be shared with other members of the class rather than as products to be submitted to a teacher for examination.

As mentioned, the goal of student-designed games is to facilitate knowledge construction, invention, and reflection. To do this, we need what Papert (1993) calls "objects-to-think-with." These objects are all those pieces of equipment such as bats and balls that students can use to construct, examine, and revise connections between old and new knowledge. It is important, then, that you are able to provide students with a wide range of equipment during the design process. Although not all equipment will be used, having a larger inventory will allow for greater creativity.

What Makes a Good Game?

One only has to read any of the blogs and communiqués among the fans of computer games to get a ready understanding of what makes a good game. In general, there are two commonly agreed-upon principles:

1. It's possible to increase in skill almost indefinitely (variety and complexity).

2. Score is directly proportional to skill for the most difficult tasks.

Bats, balls, and other pieces of equipment are the "objects-to-think-with" in games making.

Of further interest is the idea that a good game is not necessarily directly equivalent to how *fun* a multiplayer game is. As Charles Kendrick, author of *Designer's Guide to Multiplayer Quake Gameplay*, has commented:

> I tend to lose interest in any game where it's not possible to keep improving one's ability, or where improvements in ability don't show through in the game very much. If this isn't at least a little bit true of you, then ignore this document, and go back to work on your "kill everyone on the level by pressing a button." But if you're interested in creating a game with what I've defined as "good gameplay," or at least in creating a game that finds a balance between gameplay and more chaotic carnage, read on.

Essentially, Kendrick is speaking around a sense of a game being engaging. Engagement refers to the intensity and emotional quality of a person's active involvement during a task. If someone is highly engaged, we see evidence of enthusiastic participation, with high degrees of effort and positive emotion.

To be *really* engaging, an activity should

- be structured so that players can decrease or increase the level of challenge in order to match their skills,
- be easy for players to isolate the activity from other stimuli that might interfere,
- have clear performance criteria to let people know how well or poorly they are doing,
- provide concrete feedback to tell them how well they are meeting the criteria, and
- have a broad range of challenges and possibly several qualitatively different ranges of challenges.

Student-designed games fit easily into this definition. Students have the freedom to design games that match their skill levels and that have clear scoring systems that provide them with feedback. As a result, it is not unusual to see games-making lessons characterized by serious and thoughtful engagement rather than more frivolous expressions of fun. As Rovegno and Bandhauer (1994) note from their experiences with student-designed games, "The true joy and deep fun individuals experience when they learn and participate in physical activities is not expressed through sport spectator behavior. There is great joy in playing hard, doing your best, learning movement, refining technique, and meeting the challenges of the game" (page 62).

Students *do*, however, need guidance as to what constitutes a good game. These characteristics need to be explicitly presented to students. In essence, their games must

- contribute to *skill development*;
- be *safe*;
- *include, not eliminate*, students from participation (elimination makes almost no pedagogical sense when one considers that the most likely students to be eliminated are those who have the least skill and in fact need the *most* practice);
- have *high participation rates*; and
- be structured so that *all children are successful and are being challenged*.

A good game, then, is one that is *fun, fair, and safe* for all participants. By fun, we mean that the game involves participants at an appropriate level of challenge from the perspectives of both skills and strategies. By fair, we mean that the game has a good balance so that success and scoring are not too easy or too hard. That is, there is a good balance between the offense and the defense so that neither one dominates play. By safe, we mean the game has rules that keep its participants physically safe, and there are no opportunities for students to be embarrassed or humiliated.

What Student-Designed Games Are Not

First and foremost, student-designed games are not simplistic situations where you as the teacher simply explain the skill, give students some equipment, and say, "Now go make up a game." The teacher's role is critical, and as Almond (1986, page 70) notes, "The context in which you put pupils needs careful thought, the teacher must learn to intervene to support pupils doing things for themselves, and using games as a problem solving experience requires a detailed knowledge of games." As consultant, mentor, and learning resource, the teacher walks a fine balance between standing back and observing students as they create their games and intervening in the process in order to help maximize learning. Such intervention can arise with regard to keeping students safe, promoting responsible interpersonal behavior, and helping students develop their games when they reach a point where they become stuck. That is, when a game is not working because students do not have sufficient understanding of games and game strategies to solve the problem, the teacher can guide students toward workable solutions through questioning. As noted, however, teachers themselves need a good understanding of games for this to happen. Chapters 4 through 9 in this book provide a detailed account of such games knowledge.

Rovegno and Bandhauer (1994) suggest that when first exposed to student-designed games, there is the potential for teachers to possess a number of misconceptions about students' ability to design games. Five of these are included in table 1.1, together with the potential outcome of that misconception and a suggested alternative.

Getting Started With Student-Designed Games

As you read through the following chapter, you will learn about ways in which you can introduce and develop units of student-designed games. The following two chapters provide more details about the benefits of student-designed games as well as how to plan and teach them. Chapters 4 through 9 provide a host of examples of the internal workings and strategic underpinnings of games that

TABLE 1.1—Misconceptions About Student-Designed Games

Misconception	Potential outcome	Suggested alternative
All you need to do is explain the skill, give students equipment, and say, "Make up a game."	Students will focus on the skill itself rather than a component of game play.	Focus on a smaller component of a game, and build from there. (Use the templates provided in chapters 5-9 to help identify these components.)
Children understand why games have rules, boundaries, and penalties.	Children think that rules are something to follow (or break) and often argue about rules when they don't understand them. They are less likely to consider rules as tools that make a game better.	Ask significant questions during the game design process about game elements. Help develop an understanding that changing rules changes games. With older students, begin with a game and have them change it.
Children will learn strategy on their own.	Many children won't develop strategic understanding simply through game play.	Determine the strategy concept that is the focus of the lesson, and monitor the children to ensure that they remain on task; design games that enable them to learn the concept.
You cannot tell students what to do. They have to come up with it by themselves.	Games may be designed that are unsafe, or students may engage in ways in which they treat each other without respect.	Always intervene when games are not safe. Intervene also if students are being disrespectful to one another or if a conflict is getting out of hand.
You should not interrupt the planning process.	Students will rarely stop and reflect about their games unprompted.	Provide specific points within lessons where you stop the design process and allow time for critique and modification.

should allow you to set games-making tasks for your students that will allow both you and them to experience success.

In your first attempts, it is recommended that you select a game form that you know well, whether from the tag game family or those focusing on striking and fielding. Start small, do it well, and then build on it. Once you become comfortable with the curricular and instructional issues involved with student-designed games, you may wish to step further out of the box and provide students with more open-ended design challenges, to the point where they can begin to experiment with designing games that cross the traditional divide that typically characterizes various games.

References

Almond, L. (1986). Primary and secondary rules in games. In R. Thorpe, D. Bunker, & L. Almond (Eds), *Rethinking games teaching* (pp. 73-74). Loughborough, England: University of Technology.

Kendrick, C. (1997). *Designer's guide to multiplayer quake gameplay.* Available: http://planet-quake.gamespy.com/expert/qgme.html.

Papert, S. (1993). *The children's machine: Rethinking school in the age of the computer.* New York: Basic Books.

Rovegno, I., & Bandhauer, D. (1994). Child-designed games: Experience changes teachers' conceptions. *Journal of Physical Education, Recreation & Dance, 65* (6), 60-63.

CHAPTER 2

Educational Benefits of Student-Designed Games

For any new activity to be introduced into a physical education program, it must be defensible within the overall goals for the subject. In this chapter, we examine how student-designed games can contribute to a number of the components that constitute the physically educated person. In addition, the chapter outlines how games making utilizes many strategies of cooperative learning—a strategy for developing higher-order thinking and positive social behaviors. Also discussed is the idea of how games-making lessons take place in autonomy-supportive classroom environments and how these types of environments increase motivation and engagement.

Games Making and the Physically Educated Person

The International Council for Health, Physical Education, Recreation, Sport, and Dance (ICHPER•SD), in collaboration with the United Nations Educational, Scientific and Cultural Organization (UNESCO), has developed a series of goals for students in physical education settings. Using physical activity as its base, ICHPER•SD notes that the goal of physical education is to develop physically educated individuals who have the knowledge, skills, and confidence to enjoy a lifetime of healthful physical activity. These content standards have been communicated globally, and examination of a number of national curricula documents reflect their intent.

In ICHPER•SD's definition, a physically educated person meets the following seven standards:

1. Demonstrates competency in many movement forms and proficiency in a few movement forms
2. Applies movement concepts and principles to the learning and development of motor skills
3. Achieves and maintains a health-enhancing level of fitness
4. Exhibits a physically active lifestyle
5. Demonstrates responsible personal and social behavior in physical activity settings
6. Demonstrates understanding of and respect for differences among people in physical activity settings
7. Understands that physical activities provide opportunities for enjoyment, challenge, self-expression, and social interaction

This section of the chapter will examine the contribution of student-designed games to each of these outcome goals.

STANDARD 1: MOVEMENT COMPETENCY AND PROFICIENCY

The fundamental intent of this standard is the development of motor competence, with the belief that such competence will increase the likelihood of further participation into adulthood. Although students do not become involved in specific skill learning through games making, an interesting phenomenon does occur. This is one where students self-select skills that bring them success. That is, when a game has been developed that includes skills that are too difficult, students will usually modify games to make them more developmentally appropriate. Success rates during skills practice have been identified as the best predictor of final skill accomplishment. That is, the more positive practice trials a student has within a motor task (such as throwing a ball or striking a badminton shuttle), the more likely he will be to finally master that skill.

This is not to say that students will *only* design games that are easy for them. What is more likely is that they will select skills within their games that are within reach. For example, students at a school in the United Kingdom invented a game that requires throwing and catching a ball from a cut-off milk jug and handling of the ball only through the use of a swimming pool noodle. It took a number of days before the students had developed sufficient control of the jugs to enable them to play a good game. What is more relevant, however, was that everyone began at a common level. No one was favored by previous experience with the skills, and this leveling was seen as very important by students in the games-making process.

Another example of this leveling motive is that many student-designed games will also provide options for players with regard to the choice of equipment. In one Australian school where the students were developing striking and fielding games, all the games allowed for different ways for the batters to receive the ball. They could choose to hit from a tee, they could toss it to themselves, or they could receive a friendly pitch from one of their teammates. One of the fundamental tenets of developmentally appropriate practice for physical education is that teachers modify official rules, regulations, equipment, and playing space of adult sports to match the varying abilities of the children. In the case of student-designed games, students take care of this concern in ways often far superior to that of teachers. Why? Simply because they understand what they can and cannot do, and what they do and do not like, better than anyone.

STANDARD 2: KNOWLEDGE AND APPLICATION OF MOVEMENT CONCEPTS

The intent here is that students develop a cognitive understanding about motor skill performance. In this case, the process of games making takes students to the very heart of skill and tactical acquisition. By including new skills and variations of more familiar ones (e.g., finding different ways to dribble, throw, or hit), students will come to understand how games work, how different skills change the nature of a game (in terms of speed, ease, power, control, and so on), and how different rules bring about different strategic options. Concepts of effort and force, as well as spatial awareness and the concepts of directions, levels, and pathways, will be experienced in the most applied of settings.

STANDARD 3: HEALTH-ENHANCING FITNESS

This standard aims to have students develop sufficient fitness levels so that they can lead an active and healthy lifestyle. Although students are unlikely to develop games that foreground aerobic fitness or muscular strength and endurance, observations of student-designed games reveal that most of them are very inclusive and require maximum participation from all players. In particular,

Games making allows students to investigate unique tactical situations.

Small-sided games allow for higher levels of activity.

many student-designed games are played by small-sided teams. The natural consequence of this is that students in many games-making lessons should be sufficiently active to achieve a health-enhancing level of physical activity.

It should also be noted that people who have a desire to exercise—and who are confident that they can—are more likely to engage in physical fitness activities than those who lack motivation or have poor self-perception (Pan et al., 2009). The positive activity experiences that can be facilitated through well-constructed student-designed games lessons should help to increase that motivation and confidence. In schools where games making has been adopted, students who were previously disillusioned with physical activity found that enjoyment encourages them to much greater levels of physical participation in their student-designed games.

STANDARD 4: PHYSICALLY ACTIVE LIFESTYLE

The goal here is that students become aware of a number of positive emotional outcomes available as a result of participating in physical activity. These can include self-expression and social interaction as well as the development of self-confidence and a positive self-image. According to Gruber (1996) and Strong et al. (2005), positive relationships exist between children's self-esteem and physical activity as well as between their self-concept and physical activity. In games-making units, students will usually remain on the same team during both the design and playing components. The evidence on these persisting teams suggests that the following benefits are likely:

- Students have a stronger sense of control and ownership for their learning.
- Peer support and pressure within teams serve as an accountability function.

- Students who tend to disengage are not left alone.
- Students learn to help each other—to give help and to accept it.

It is hoped these positive experiences will then transfer to a more affirmative approach to participation in other physical activity settings.

STANDARD 5: PERSONAL AND SOCIAL BEHAVIOR

The intent of this standard is one of achieving self-initiated behaviors that promote personal and group success in activity settings. These behaviors include safe practices, adherence to rules and procedures, etiquette, cooperation and teamwork, ethical behavior in sport, and positive social interaction. The very essence of games making contributes powerfully to this goal. By requiring a more sophisticated understanding of the collaborative climate required to create and play good games, games-making lessons can help students learn about and achieve the social conditions necessary for positive interactions and cooperation. Although Rovegno and Bandhauer (1994) note that arguments and humiliating situations are not eliminated in student-designed games, they have observed there is less fighting and fewer embarrassing situations in these lessons because, as the students have said, they have the freedom to design and modify their games.

STANDARD 6: UNDERSTANDING OF AND RESPECT FOR INDIVIDUAL DIFFERENCES

The intent of this standard is that students will interact positively with others in their class regardless of personal differences (e.g., race, gender, ability, disability, culture, ethnicity, religion) and can recognize similarities and differences between and among people that can contribute to cooperative and competitive activities.

Well-presented games-making lessons can help students understand and appreciate the importance of fair play.

One of the key features of student-designed games is that some of the most creative ideas are offered by those who are not the most skilled. In this sense, those students can be appreciated for a contribution to physical education that would not always be available in other competitive situations. As previously noted, students tend not to design games that are too difficult to play or are exclusionary. This would suggest an awareness of the concept of fairness and inclusion.

STANDARD 7: PERSONAL MEANING DERIVED FROM PHYSICAL ACTIVITY

The intent of this standard is the establishment of patterns of regular participation in meaningful physical activity, and for students to continue being physically active beyond the lessons in which they participate at school. It is important to note that voluntary participation often develops from the initial enjoyment that is derived from the activity coupled with the requisite skills needed for participation. Consequently, students are more likely to participate if they have opportunities to develop interests that are personally meaningful to them. Given that games making provides students with high degrees of choice and allows for experimentation, it only follows that many students across a number of grade levels and schools report very positively about their experiences in student-designed games units.

Games Making and Cooperative Learning

When students design games, they do so in an environment that requires collaboration, tolerance, respect for others, and the sharing of ideas. In essence, the learning setting is one that focuses on *cooperation* rather than competition. In cooperative learning, students work together in small groups to complete group tasks, and a central feature is that the members of the group will help each other

Enjoyment coupled with sufficient skills is a prerequisite for voluntary participation.

learn while achieving the group goals. Cooperative learning is a recognized strategy for creating learning gains and developing higher-order thinking, positive social behavior, and peer acceptance (Cohen, 1994). It involves pupils working in small groups that have been deliberately selected by their teacher to ensure that they are fair and free from both close friendships and strong rivalries. Research on cooperative learning has found that it can result in the development of positive relationships between classmates, improved social skills, a longer retention of what is learned, improved higher-level reasoning and critical thinking skills, higher levels of creativity, and more positive attitudes toward the subject matter (Gillies, 2007; Johnson, Johnson, & Johnson-Holubec, 1998). However, in order to be teaching cooperatively, a practitioner needs to obtain five outcomes: positive interdependence, individual accountability, group processing, face-to-face interaction, and shared group goals. Games making, by its very nature, contains the key pedagogical context for learning through cooperation. The teacher's role is to act as a facilitator by moving from group to group to monitor the learning process. The teacher also provides students with ongoing feedback and assessment of the group's progress.

Games Making and Student Motivation and Engagement

In any classroom, a teacher will use a number of strategies to motivate students to achieve their potential. Although this is the case across schooling, any one teacher's management style can range between one that is controlling and directive, through to one that is more autonomy supportive. Figure 2.1 shows this comparison.

Research on class climates has shown that when a class is oriented more toward autonomy support, this fosters creativity, long-term persistence, and conceptual understanding (high-quality learning). The same holds true in physical education, where higher-autonomy climates are associated with high intrinsic motivation, persistence, interest, and participation (Carpenter & Morgan, 1999).

The key elements of games-making lessons would see them as having a high-autonomy focus. Students are presented with open challenges (design a new game), are provided with choices (selection of equipment, playing space, and

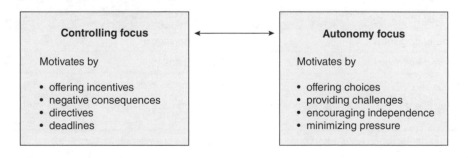

FIGURE 2.1 **Continuum of teacher control.**
Based on J. Reeve et al., 2004, "Enhancing students' engagement by increasing teachers' autonomy support," *Motivation and Emotion* 28 (2): 147-169.

rules), and are allowed to follow the process of game design in a way that suits them. With reference to this last point, some groups will prefer to have all their ideas about equipment and rules settled before they start to play, while others prefer to begin by playing and then make modifications as they face challenges. The important issue is that in an autonomy-supportive climate, the teacher accommodates both these changes and does not pressure students to reach strict predetermined timelines. In addition, as Ledingham and Cox (1989) note, there can be no preordained end product to any games-making lesson, only a process to which you wish to expose the students. The success of the lesson really depends upon how the teacher can provide an environment in which the students do not feel obligated to produce something for her.

Engagement is a broad construct that reflects a person's enthusiastic participation in a task (Reeve et al., 2004). Although *participation* is a term that refers to taking part, *engagement* is a stronger term that includes the intensity and emotional quality of a person's active involvement. So while a person may indeed be participating, he can be minimally engaged or actively involved. Table 2.1 shows some comparisons.

Engagement, then, is an important idea because it has been shown to predict important outcomes such as achievement and whether students will remain in school or drop out. The key link from the perspective of games making is that engagement is related to class climate. That is, as teachers use more autonomy support during instruction, their students are more engaged.

Conclusion

This chapter has shown how participation in games making can help students achieve many of the aspects of the physically educated person. By enabling participation in a cooperative, creative, and autonomy-supportive environment, when taught well, student-designed games can produce a form of physical education that sees students as motivated and highly engaged participants. The next chapter in this text explains how to design and organize student-designed games lessons so that they are, indeed, taught well.

TABLE 2.1—Characteristics of Minimally and Highly Engaged Students	
Minimally engaged	**Highly engaged**
Dispersed attention	Focused attention
Passive, slow, minimal effort	Active, quick, intense effort
Verbally silent (does not ask questions or discuss)	Verbally participating (asks questions and discusses)
Gives up easily (decreases effort over time)	Persists (increases effort over time)
Flat emotive tone (appears bored or disinterested)	Positive emotive tone (shows enjoyment, interest, and fun)

References

Carpenter, P., & Morgan, K. (1999). Motivational climate, personal goal perspectives, and cognitive and affective responses in physical education classes. *European Journal of Physical Education, 4,* 31-44.

Cohen, E.G. (1994). *Designing groupwork: Strategies for the heterogeneous classroom.* New York: Teachers College, Columbia University.

Gillies, R.M. (2007). *Cooperative learning: Integrating theory and practice.* Los Angeles: SAGE.

Gruber, J.J. (1996). Physical activity and self-esteem development in children. In G.A. Stull & H.M. Eckert (Eds.), *The Academy papers.* Champaign, IL: Human Kinetics.

Johnson, D.W., Johnson, R.T., & Johnson-Holubec, E. (1998). *Cooperation in the classroom.* (7th ed.). Edina, MN: Interaction Book.

Ledingham, D., & Cox, R.L. (1989). Games-making evaluated. *Scottish Journal of Physical Education, 17* (3), 14; 16.

Pan, S.Y., Cameron, C., DesMeules, M., Morrison, H., Craig, C.L., & Jiang, X.H. (2009). Individual, social, environmental, and physical environmental correlates with physical activity among Canadians: A cross-sectional study. *BMC Public Health, 9* (21) (16 January 2009).

Reeve, J., Jang, H., Carrell, D., Jeon, S., & Barch, J. (2004). Enhancing students' engagement by increasing teachers' autonomy support. *Motivation and Emotion, 28* (2), 147-169.

Rovegno, I., & Bandhauer, D. (1994). Child-designed games: Experience changes teachers' conceptions. *Journal of Physical Education, Recreation & Dance, 65* (6), 60-63.

Strong, W.B., Malina, R.M., Blimkie, C.J., Daniels, S.R., Dishman, R.K., Gutin, B., et al. (2005). Evidence-based physical activity for school-age youth. *Journal of Pediatrics, 146* (6), 732-737.

CHAPTER 3

Instructional Strategies for Games Making

As mentioned in chapter 1, teaching student-designed games is not simply a case of the teacher explaining a skill, handing out equipment, and saying, "Make up a game." There is a significant amount of planning involved, and without this planning the outcomes will be less than anticipated. There is also the need for active teaching. It is just that this teaching is more away from center stage, with the focus being on helping students to be successful in small mixed-ability learning groups. If you were to imagine that the lesson had three stages—before, during, and after the lesson—then most of the teacher's work would be done in the before and after sections to ensure that the student-designed games reached their potential. The "during" is a time of facilitating, as the students take the lead.

The purpose of this chapter is to take you through a sequence of events that work to create a successful games-making experience for students. It deals with both planning and implementation issues and covers both managerial and instructional tasks. A diagram of the planning and implementation process is presented in figure 3.1.

Play end product

Allow time for revision

Allow for playing time

Allow for planning time

Present the challenge

Organize learning groups

Decide on game type

Determine outcome goal

FIGURE 3.1   The planning and implementation process for student-designed games.

Choose Outcome Goals

The first task when planning a games-making unit is to decide what you want the students to achieve as a result of their experiences. This will depend upon the students' grade level, their experience with games (and particularly their experience with exploring games tactics), and their experience with games making.

There are a number of different goals of games making, and you have to decide which of these you want to focus upon. Some of these include the following:

- Finding out why rules are important and what purpose they serve
- Constructing completely new games
- Sharing ideas and working cooperatively
- Teaching others
- Actively engaging with and exploring components of game play (skills and strategy)
- Thinking critically about games experiences outside of class and school

Decide Type of Game and Student Choice

Once the main goals of the unit have been determined, two questions arise. These are (1) what *type* of game do you want the students to design, and (2) how much *choice* do you plan on giving students in designing their games?

The first case will relate to the type of game problem you want students to explore. It might be specific, such as exploring the effects of boundaries in tag games or hitting to a space in striking and fielding games. On the other hand, it might be more general, as in exploring the key tactics and strategies of net games and wall games. Chapter 4 provides a detailed account of the different game forms and the key tactical features of each one.

In answering the second question, you have a number of options, with each allowing an increased level of autonomy for the students. These include the *structured approach*, the *limited-choice approach*, and the *open-choice approach*.

STRUCTURED APPROACH

The structured approach is the most teacher-controlled version of games making and involves limiting the number of choices available to the students. The most common limits include designating the playing space and the number of players on each team as well as the equipment that is available to the games designers. Cox (1988) suggests that in this format, the choice of equipment be limited to about five items. The advantage of the structured approach is that games are usually developed quite quickly, and they are not overly complicated. The trade-off for simplicity, of course, is that many of the games look the same.

Another version of the structured approach is to present students with a game, and following a period of play, allow them to make changes to the number of players, the size of the court or field, the implements or balls used, or other simple rules. The game of indoor flickerball is used as an example here.

Indoor flickerball is a noncontact sport, played on a basketball court with an American football, by two teams of anywhere between four and eight players on each side. The aim of the game is to throw the football from within the 3-point area so that it goes through the goal. This is worth 3 points. A shot that hits the ring (but does not travel through) is worth 2, while a shot hitting only the backboard scores 1.

Players can hold the ball for only five seconds and may not walk or run while in possession of the ball. However, whenever the ball hits the ground the team who was last in possession loses that possession. That is, if a player from the red team knocks down a pass from one blue player to another, the red team gains possession.

In the structured option, you will first play flickerball in its original form and then ask students what modifications they might like to include. These can include the following:

- Allow running with the ball. (For so many steps? Unlimited? How can you stop a player running?)
- Shoot from anywhere, not just inside the 3-point line. (Do the score values change?)
- Whenever the ball hits the ground, the team to touch it last loses possession.
- The team that gains control must first make a lateral or backward pass (i.e., the player cannot shoot immediately).

As the teacher, you can choose to focus on one rule after each series of play (e.g., shooting in the 3-point zone for the first session, then running rules in the next), or you can allow input from the students concerning any of the rules of the game. These rule changes can be tested for a short period of play and then either adopted permanently or students may choose to revert to the original rule.

LIMITED-CHOICE APPROACH

In the limited-choice approach, students will work in small teams to decide upon one particular aspect of the game. For a net or wall game, one group might decide on the paddle or racket to be used, while another group will decide on the serving rules. Still another group will be discussing ways in which the ball can (or cannot) be sent over the net.

The technique best used in this limited-choice approach is known as the *jigsaw classroom*, and the underlying theory is that just as in a jigsaw puzzle, each piece—each student's part—is essential for the completion and full understanding of the final product. If each student's part is essential, then each student is essential; and that is precisely what makes this strategy so effective. The following capsule gives an example of how the jigsaw classroom works.

The students in a history class are divided into small groups of five or six students each, and their task is to learn about World War II. In one jigsaw group, Trey is responsible for researching Hitler's rise to power in prewar Germany. Another member of the group, Mandy, is assigned to cover concentration camps. Pedro is assigned Britain's role in the war, Melody is to research the contribution of the Soviet Union, and Tyrone will handle Japan's entry into the war. Finally, Clara will read about the development of the atom bomb.

Eventually each student will come back to the jigsaw group and will try to present a well-organized report to the group. The situation is specifically structured so that the only access any member has to the other five assignments is by listening closely to the report of the person reciting. Thus, if Tyrone doesn't like Pedro, or if he thinks Mandy is a nerd and tunes her out or makes fun of her, he cannot possibly do well on the test that follows.

To increase the chances that each report will be accurate, the students doing the research do not immediately take their reports back to their jigsaw groups. Instead, they meet first with students who have the identical assignment (one from each jigsaw group). For example, students assigned to the atom bomb topic meet as a team of specialists, gathering information, becoming experts on their topic, and rehearsing their presentations. We call this the "expert" group. It is particularly useful for students who might have initial difficulty learning or organizing their part of the assignment, for it allows them to hear and rehearse with other "experts."

In a jigsaw games lesson, students from different teams will meet to design the primary rules of a particular game. After these "rules experts" have made their decision, they then return to their original teams to put the game together. In this way, all final games should be the same across groups. If a game is not developed consistently with the model, it will be as a result of that particular expert's lack of understanding or inattention during the design phase. That student is thereby accountable to the entire group.

Let's consider another jigsaw example: Students are charged with designing a tag game. The expert designers in this situation will determine the rules about the following:

- Boundaries and playing area
- How to tag (where, equipment, safety)
- How to get "unfrozen" after being tagged
- Safe zones (places where you may not be tagged)
- Chasing limitations (how to move, whether you can dive after someone to tag them)

Once these rules have been decided, the players return and experiment with the game.

In the jigsaw method, students will make decisions about a single component of a game.

Provide Time to Play

In addition to planning and experimenting within teams, it is also important to give the students opportunities to see their games played. Although a small-sided game such as a two-versus-two net game could be practiced within the design team, games that require more players will need the participation of other teams.

When other teams play their game, the design team will get a fresh view of their game. New players might find new strategic answers to the games challenges, and they may also find loopholes. It is not always smooth sailing, however. Student designers often become frustrated when others play their game. Although the players who have designed their game have a good understanding and know it intimately, and they know the nuances of why the rules are as they appear, when they present to others there is more often than not some confusion about rule interpretations. The confusion can be caused by three situations: first, if the game is poorly explained; second, if the presenting team officiates the game poorly; and third, if a situation arises in a game for which no rule has yet been established. However, the process of fine-tuning and learning about games that comes from playing far outweighs the frustrations associated with game presentation.

The problem of poor game explanation usually arises when a team tries to explain each and every finite rule. This becomes unwieldy to the extent that many of the key rules are forgotten before play even begins. To help students present their game in succinct but inclusive form, the script in figure 3.3 acts as a good starting point. All the students need to do is fill in the blanks from their game (an example is shown in figure 3.4).

Review

Once teams have had a chance to see their games in action, coupled with any new rules that had to be incorporated during the play phase, they can once again review their games to put the finishing touches on the product. This final product can then be presented in written form.

At Ripon Grammar, each team created a wiki in which their wiki manager recorded the progress of the game. This allowed the teacher (and other invited participants) to make suggestions and contributions to the game as it was being designed. The wiki also allowed the students to work on their game outside of class time and to share ideas with their friends. Students were also able to look at other groups' work outside of class time in order to get ideas and have internal critique. This use of other students' ideas is not considered plagiarism but more a positive analysis. It was not simply direct copying of games, but interaction lent to original thought as well as individual accountability for the product as a team.

The nature of wikis is that an e-mail alert is sent to all participants each time the Web page has been edited. Such was the enthusiasm created by this technology that within the first week of the presentation of the games-making assignment, there were a total of 86 interactions and edits to the six Web sites.

Being located in an online environment also meant that students from a school in Alabama played the games and made suggestions about rules. In a number of cases, ideas of the American contingent could be evaluated, critiqued, and

The name of this game is _____.

The aim of the game is to *[outline the scoring goal]* _____
_____
_____.

You do this by _____
_____
_____.

The attacking team is allowed to _____
_____, _____
_____, and _____
_____.

They are not allowed to _____
_____, _____
_____, or _____
_____.

The defensive team is allowed to _____
_____, _____
_____, and _____
_____.

They are not allowed to _____
_____, _____
_____, or _____
_____.

If the attacking team breaks one of the "allowed things," then _____
_____
_____.

If the defensive team breaks a rule, the penalty is _____
_____
_____.

The boundaries of the court are marked by *[show them]*_____
_____

and if the ball goes out, then _____
_____.

From P. Hastie, 2010, *Student-Designed Games: Strategies for Promoting Creativity, Cooperation, and Skill Development* (Champaign, IL: Human Kinetics).

FIGURE 3.3   **Script for explaining game rules.**

The name of this game is _run the gauntlet_.

The aim of the game is to _capture the flag and then get it back over your end line_.

You do this by _first scoring a try, then picking up the cone and running fast back home without getting hit by the ball_.

The attacking team is allowed to _pass the ball in any direction, but all passes must be in the air (no drops)_.

They are not allowed to _run with the ball, pass the flag once they get it, or make contact with the defenders when they are trying to hit the flag carrier._

The defensive team is allowed to _intercept passes and run with the ball to half-court when they are trying to hit the flag carrier on counterattack_.

They are not allowed to _make contact with the ball carrier, knock the ball out of his hands, or run with the ball past half-court on counterattack_.

If the attacking team breaks one of the "allowed things," _then the other team gets possession from the point of the error (e.g., dropped pass)_.

If the defensive team breaks a rule, the penalty is _either a free throw on attack or a score on counterattack_.

The boundaries of the court are marked by _4 orange cones, with the end zones being indicated by the blue cones_, and if the ball goes out, _then the other team gets possession for a throw-in_.

FIGURE 3.4   **Sample filled-out script for explaining game rules for run the gauntlet.**

adopted (or not) by the designers of the parent game. The wiki allowed a dialogue through questioning from the English students to these outside participants. In addition, photographs were uploaded onto the wiki that showed how the American students played the games.

The Role of the Teacher

The teacher has important managerial and teaching roles during the games-making process. Importantly, that task is _not_ to stand back and do nothing, but to use questioning skills to ask students to clarify their games, to explain their rules, and to provide suggestions (which may or may not be adopted). The challenge is to be a facilitator, not a director, and to avoid being critical.

The use of questioning rather than direction is recommended when dealing with conflict between students.

WHEN TO INTERVENE

There will be times, however, when direct intervention is necessary. Your first role must be to ensure safety. If students have included a component within a game that is dangerous, then it is your responsibility to point this out and help students find a safe alternative. You should also intervene if students are being disrespectful to one another or if a conflict is getting out of hand. Rovegno and Bandhauer (1994) comment that although there is less fighting and fewer embarrassing situations because students have the freedom to design and modify their games, arguments and humiliating situations can and do emerge. The key here is to try to discover the underlying causes for these problems, which are usually the result of frustration from a lack of understanding (while playing games) or strong differences of opinion in the design phase.

ASSISTING IN THE GROUP WORK PROCESS

Teachers also need to be involved in the group work process, not so much to direct the conversations and planning, but more to check that all students have an input into their games and are making contributions. Rovegno et al. (1995) list four situations where teachers might legitimately interrupt in the group process. These are (1) ensuring that all students get an opportunity to speak and provide input, (2) ensuring all students listen to the input of others, (3) checking for understanding, and (4) helping students ask each other questions.

Although these four situations are aimed at helping students work as a complete team, teachers also need to be aware of potential coasting. In coasting, one or a few students do the bulk of the work, and the others take a free ride to ensure that their participation levels are as low as possible.

ASSISTING DURING MATCH PLAY

Although the need for safety is vital, the experience of refereeing a game is also vital for students if they are going to fully understanding the game that has been created. In run the gauntlet, one of the three groups was always the match official group. They were responsible for managing all aspects of match play, including rule queries. The teacher, in this case, allowed his students to interpret the rules of the game and enforce them in match play. He believed that his job was to let them make mistakes and refrain from overriding the students' decisions.

He also thought it was vital for him to understand the game at least as well as his students so that he could ask relevant questions at pertinent times to ensure that arguments and humiliating situations were quickly and peacefully resolved.

Conclusion

As noted in the introduction to this chapter, giving students the freedom and autonomy to design their own games does not take the teacher out of a pedagogical role. It's just different from more direct instruction. The keys for successful games making include the teacher's

- specifying the instructional objectives;
- making preinstructional decisions;
- allocating teams, time, resources available, and assessment;
- communicating task objectives and task structure;
- setting the cooperative assignment in motion;
- monitoring the cooperative learning groups and intervening as necessary; and
- evaluating learning.

References

Cox, R.L. (1988). Games-making: Principles and procedures. *Scottish Journal of Physical Education, 16* (2), 14-16.

Rovegno, I., & Bandhauer, D. (1994). Child-designed games: Experience changes teachers' conceptions. *Journal of Physical Education, Recreation & Dance, 65* (6), 60-63.

Rovegno, I., Skonie, R., Charpenel, T., & Sieving, J. (1995). Learning to teach critical thinking through child-designed games. *Teaching Elementary Physical Education, 6* (1), 1; 6; 15.

CHAPTER 4

Understanding Games

The purpose of this chapter is to provide a more complete description of what we mean by games and game play. It will also help you to understand how the rest of the book is organized in terms of the way games can be grouped into different categories. Understanding the essential features of games and how they can be classified allows us to ask questions that will help students to design fun, challenging, and engaging games of their own.

What Is a Game?

Suits (1978) offers a rather complex definition of a game, but it does provide us with a good base from which to understand our topic. According to Suits, to participate in a game is to attempt to achieve a specific state of affairs, using only means permitted by rules, where the rules prohibit use of more efficient in favor of less efficient means, and where such rules are accepted just because they make possible such activity (Suits, 1978, page 41).

Suits' definition outlines four conditions that must all be present in order that an activity can be labeled as a game. Each of these will now be examined in more detail, and examples will be given to help explain the key concepts.

ALL GAMES HAVE A GOAL

When Suits speaks of "a specific state of affairs," he is referring to the goal of the game. The goal here is not winning, per se, but it relates more to a situation where players use their skills to achieve a particular *end point*. In badminton, that end point arrives when the shuttle has landed on the court of the opponent, while the end point in soccer is when the ball goes into the goal. Consequently, the skill required of the badminton player is to strike the shuttle over a net to a point where the opponent cannot return it, while soccer players must kick the ball with their feet or strike it with their heads away from the defenders and past the goalkeeper.

Photo courtesy of Cedric Schweingruber.

All games have a goal.

ALL GAMES HAVE RULES

The second necessary condition is that a game must have rules, and these rules provide both *descriptive* and *defining* frameworks for how the goal is to be achieved. The *descriptive* framework describes the setup of the game and its equipment, while the *defining* framework stipulates what means of play are required and permitted. In volleyball, for example, the descriptive framework refers to the measurement of the court, the net and its height, and the type of ball that is used. The defining framework of volleyball is that the ball is not allowed to touch the ground and that you are allowed three hits to send the ball over the net.

The descriptive and defining frameworks (i.e., rules) also serve to differentiate between different games. As an example, what defines handball as handball and not basketball are those rules that describe how you can move with the ball and run with it in ways that are not possible in basketball. The defining rules of softball list the ways the ball must be sent to the batter, which differentiates it from baseball and rounders, other sports whose goal is to hit the ball with a stick and run around a series of bases.

ALL GAMES HAVE RESTRICTIONS

Games will also include rules about what is *not allowed* in the course of play. Nearly all games include rules that favor *less* efficient over more efficient ways to achieve the goal. Indeed, sometimes the most logical and easiest solution is not available. Take soccer for example. Most of us would agree it would be easier to throw the ball into the goal than to kick it. However, if this were the case, soccer would cease to be soccer and would become handball. How often during a game of golf do you wish you could kick the ball from behind a tree or throw it out of a bunker or over a water hazard?

As Suits quotes, "In anything but a game, the gratuitous introduction of unnecessary obstacles to the achievement of an end is regarded as a decidedly irrational thing to do, whereas in games it appears to be an absolutely essential thing to do" (Suits, 1978, page 39). And so these limits are put in games in order to make them fun and challenging. Whereas in work and daily life we try to avoid all unnecessary obstacles, in games we do exactly the opposite.

Huizinga (1950, page 13) also comments how games and play move outside our ordinary lives:

Summing up the formal characteristics of play we might call it a free activity standing quite consciously outside "ordinary" life as being "not serious," but at the same time absorbing the player intensely and utterly. It is an activity connected with no material interest, and no profit can be gained by it. It proceeds within its own proper boundaries of time and space according to fixed rules and in an orderly manner. It promotes the formation of social groupings which tend to surround themselves with secrecy and to stress their difference from the world by disguise or other means.

Sometimes we don't stick to the rules!

Photo courtesy of Samantha Endicott.

The descriptive and defining frameworks, together with a game's restrictions, make up a game's *constitutive rules*: those that define all of the circumstances that must be satisfied when participating in a game. That is, constitutive rules delineate the means that must, can, and cannot be employed in pursuit of the goal of the game.

GAMES REQUIRE THE ACCEPTANCE OF RULES BY THE PLAYERS

The fourth necessary condition to legitimize a game is the acceptance of the constitutive rules. Unless all players are operating from the same set of rules and agree to these, the game cannot exist. Although fair play is defined as conduct that adheres to the rules, it is still preceded by the acceptance of these rules in spirit so as to make the game possible. How often do backyard games break down because of disputes over the agreed-upon rules?

So all games must fulfill the four conditions. There must be a goal, rules that provide the framework of the game, rules that restrict what people can do in order to provide challenge from both thinking and physical perspectives, and players who are in accord when they play the game. When students design their own games, it is useful for them to begin by thinking of these conditions. In chapters 5 through 9 there are templates aimed at helping students think about how to develop a game's goal and its constitutive rules.

Classifying Games

This section will outline how we have come to think about games in this book. Before we start, however, it is necessary to provide a limit on what we will be discussing. Playing chess qualifies within Suits' definition of a game. In chess, the goal is to capture your opponent's king, players alternate turns, and certain pieces can be moved only in specific directions. For a game of chess to be played, both participants need to concur with the common rules.

On the other hand, chess is a game in which the demonstration of motor competency plays no bearing on the outcome. The same is the case with card games such as solitaire or poker, board games such as Monopoly, or word games such as Scrabble. For the remainder of this book, a specific rule will apply: A game will be included only if its goal can be achieved by demonstrating a degree of motor competency.

OUTCOME GOAL

We know all games begin with a goal, and the first divide is whether or not that goal will involve an opponent. Figure 4.1 shows sample games in each category.

Games that are noncompetitive are those in which an opponent is absent. However, these games are not necessarily limited to play by an individual (such as hopscotch). The popular Israeli beach game of matkot involves players using a paddle to volley a small rubber ball back and forth. The goal of this game is to keep the rally going as long as possible. Other noncompetitive games are presented in chapter 11 of this book.

It is also common in the green spaces of universities or colleges to see players throwing a Frisbee to each other. This form of Frisbee still qualifies as a game because the goal is to send the disc to someone without it hitting the ground, and there are unsaid rules accepted among the players that limit how the Frisbee can travel. The easiest way to send a Frisbee to a friend would simply be to walk up to the person and hand it over. The restrictive element that makes it a game is the rule that you have to throw the disc over a long distance so the receiver does not have to move far to catch it, or that the catcher has to vigorously chase it.

Competitive games, on the other hand, will involve an opponent. That opponent is in a position where she is trying to achieve the same goal as you are, usually either before you or more times over a certain period.

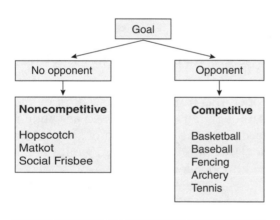

FIGURE 4.1 **Games may or may not involve the use of an opponent.**

COMPETITIVE ASPECT

Competitive games can be categorized in two ways. The first of these we call *interactive* because there is an offense that is trying to score and a defense that is actively working against you in pursuit of your goal. In basketball, while you are trying to get the ball into the goal, your opponent is first trying to get possession of the ball so you cannot score, and if this is not possible, is trying to make your shot on the basket as difficult as possible. In table tennis, both you and your opponent are trying to hit the ball so it cannot be returned. Each of you will hit with spin, hit the ball to different parts of the table, or change the speed of the ball. In baseball, while you are trying to hit the ball to an open space, the pitcher is trying to throw the ball so you cannot hit it, or if you can, so that you hit it directly to the fielders.

The second category of competitive games is that of *noninteractive games*. In these games, the player's or team's pursuit of the game's goal is independent of and inconsequential to another player's or team's pursuit of the same goal. Playing darts or golf are examples of these noninteractive games, also referred to as *parallel tests* (Hardman et al., 1996). In noninteractive games, players perform in isolation against an existing standard on a movement task and hence have some sense of competing against others. Nonetheless, it is the standard attained by the other competitors that they strive to better, rather than conquering the opponent per se.

LEVEL OF INTERCEPTION

The interactive competitive games category can be further divided according to the nature of that interaction (figure 4.2). This refers essentially to the privileges and limits given to the offense and defense.

In *direct interceptive games*, a defensive player can have an absolute impact on an opposing player or the ball. That is, defenders can legally impose themselves between the attacking players and their end point in order to restrict their achievement of the game's goal.

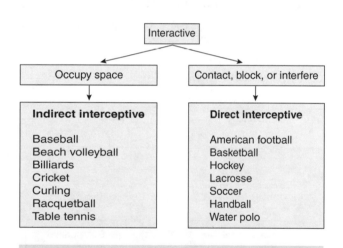

FIGURE 4.2 **Interactive competitive games can be classified by the nature of interaction.**

The characteristics of direct interceptive activities are listed as follows:

- Opponents occupy the same defined area of play simultaneously and usually in equal numbers.
- Opponents generally compete for the space on the field of play.
- In defense, direct interception occurs through
  - body contact (e.g., American or Australian football and rugby),
  - blocking the passage of an opponent (e.g., handball), or
  - stealing possession of the implement of play while it is being manipulated by the opponent (e.g., hockey).

- In offense, direct interception occurs through
  - avoiding or using the opponent's interceptive behavior or
  - controlling the implements of play (e.g., the ball and field space).

In *indirect interceptive games*, there is no allowance for contact, blocking, or interference. All that is possible is for players to either intercept the implements of play or occupy space critical to their opponents. In billiards or curling, for example, it is possible to place one's equipment in the space desired by your opponent in order to obstruct the path to any possible target for your opponent. In volleyball, a team may put up a block to take away the space where the opposing team wants to spike the ball. In softball, the fielding team will take up the space where the ball is most likely to be hit by the batter. What you cannot do in softball is directly block your opponent's pathway. That is, you cannot tackle or block the runners as they progress around the bases. In badminton, although a player can direct the movement of an opponent by hitting the shuttle to a certain place, he cannot physically block the opponent's pathway to the shuttle.

THE COMPLETE PICTURE

Figure 4.3 shows the final derivation of the games tree. All games begin with a goal and then disperse according to the constitutive rules that govern them. In all cases, however, there must be an accord among the participants to partake within the spirit of these rules.

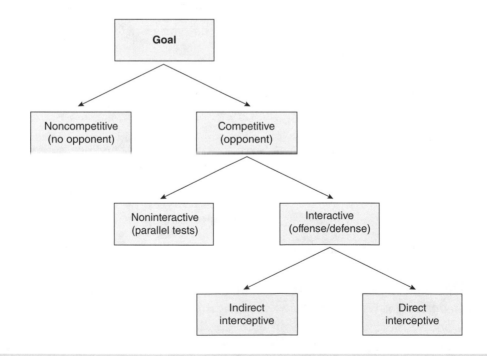

FIGURE 4.3   The games tree.

Classifying Games According to Their Tactics

As noted earlier, the goals and rules of a game provide it with its structure and form, and from the goals and rules, specific tactics then become available or unavailable to the players. Although it would be possible to continue this book with an examination of games that belong to each of the categories shown in figure 4.3 in order to help students in their understanding of games, we have found it more appropriate to consider the tactical commonalities among games.

Thinking about games in terms of what tactics they stimulate is considered the most appropriate way to group games. This is because tactical awareness can be taught as concepts that transfer between games within a group. When taking into consideration all the games we currently know, together with those yet to be designed, games researchers have designated five categories. These are *tag games, target games, invasion games, striking and fielding games,* and *net and wall games*. All of the games within a category will have a similar tactical underpinning. To help us understand this, we first need to be able to discriminate between primary and secondary rules.

PRIMARY RULES

Primary rules are those that identify how the game is played and how to win. They provide a game's essential character and what distinguishes it from another. Grehaigne, Richard, and Griffin (2005) list the methods of scoring and players' rights as two components of all primary rules.

- **Methods of scoring.** *Primary rules* will dictate the necessary skills for scoring. A primary rule of volleyball is that you must volley the ball with your body (versus using a racket), while in soccer players can use only their feet and heads to transfer the ball while inside the field of play (they can throw it in from the sideline). These rules make volleyball different from badminton and soccer different from handball, where you can throw the ball into the goal.

- **Players' rights.** In all games, players will have rights from both an offensive and defensive standpoint. As mentioned, in the noninteractive games you cannot limit the movement of the players. While in handball, you can take three steps with the ball, in games such as netball and ultimate Frisbee you cannot move at all. In basketball you can only move with the ball while dribbling. In rugby you can pick up the ball and run with it, but you are limited to only passing backward.

SECONDARY RULES

Secondary rules are those that arise out of the experience of playing a game. These are rules that can be changed without affecting the essential character of the game. For example, the tie-break in tennis varies according to the competition league in which it is adopted. Similarly, the height of the net in volleyball differs in men's and women's competitions and is also dependent upon the age of the competitors. The shot clock in basketball is a secondary rule that limits the time a team has before it must make a shot attempt, and in every level of competition, the time of the shot clock differs. In international and both men's and women's professional basketball, the shot clock is set at 24 seconds. However, in intercollegiate play in the United States, the time is 35 seconds in the men's game and 30 seconds for women.

When designing games, students will need to first determine the goal of a game and outline its primary rules. From that point, however, they can then experiment extensively with the secondary rules to adjust them for their skill levels, as well as the equipment and space available, in order to make them the most fun and engaging. It should be noted at this point that rules of all the game samples presented in this book are not set in stone, and in none of the games are there specific court dimensions, net heights, bat sizes (or types), or the ball to be used. Everything is simply a sample of a game that works and is fun for the participants. Each group playing one of these games has full liberty to change it to maximize their own enjoyment and challenge.

HOW RULES AFFECT PLAY

Let's use the game of argoball as an example of how changing the secondary rules can alter a game. The goal of argoball is to hit a ball into space and then run from the home base to an end base and back without getting tagged with the ball by a defensive player. The primary rules of this game are that the ball must be hit forward, the pitch must be a friendly toss to the batter, and regardless of whether the ball is hit or not, the batter must leave the batter's box and run. Further, a batter cannot wait in the end base while the next player bats, but can stay in there waiting for the most opportune time to run.

Table 4.1 gives an excellent example of how changing a certain component of the game will change the underlying skills and tactics being used while maintaining the essential character of argoball.

Tag Games

In all tag games, the fundamental goal is to tag an opponent while avoiding being tagged yourself. Tag games can be divided into two types—the one-on-one combative games such as fencing, kendo, and other martial arts, as well as the chasing, fleeing, and dodging games so common in physical education and free play time (table 4.2 on page 41).

Target Games

The fundamental goal of target games is to place your object closest to the key point on the playing area, be it a board as in darts or archery, or to hit objects as in bowling. From table 4.3 on page 41 you can see these games are divided into those where there is direct opposition (where you can occupy the critical space of an opponent) and where players are independent of each other and you have no effect on them.

TABLE 4.1—Possible Rule Modifications for Argoball

Game modification	Expected outcomes
NUMBER OF PLAYERS	
3 defenders	• More running than passing for defense. • Defense worries about chasing offense. • Defense worries about field placement. • Scoring goes up, outs go down. • Offense moves up and down the field more easily. • The batting roster cycles through faster. • Less precise thinking required for offense. • More fatigue for defense.
10 defenders	• More passing than running. • Scoring goes down, outs go up. • Game as a whole slows down. • Fewer fast breaks. • More calculation and planning required for the offense. • Batting roster does not cycle through as fast. • Offense moves less quickly. • Fewer times that offense makes it back to batter's box. • Less fatigue for defense.
BALL TYPE	
Small ball versus large	• A small ball (e.g., tennis ball, racquetball) is more difficult to catch, field, and hit but is easier to throw. • A medium ball (e.g., softball, volleyball) is easier to catch, field, hit, and throw. • A large ball (e.g., beach ball, large playground ball) is easy to hit and field but harder to throw and catch and won't travel as far.
Light versus heavy	• A light ball is harder to throw and hit. • A light ball is easier to move with than a heavy ball. • A light ball will not go as far when hit, so it is harder on the runner. • A heavy ball is not as safe but is harder for the defense to catch and throw. • A light ball brings the scores down, while a heavy ball brings the scores up.
Bouncy versus nonbouncy	• A bouncy ball makes the defense work harder to catch the ball on the first hit. • A nonbouncy ball is easier to catch. • A bouncy ball moves the game faster, while a nonbouncy ball slows the game down.
BAT SHAPE AND SIZE	
	• A bigger bat increases the likelihood of hitting the ball. • A lighter bat is easier to swing than a heavy one. • A baseball bat is harder to hit with than a tennis racket. • Using an arm or leg to hit or kick the ball is more predictable than a bat or racket. • A light tennis racket provides higher success rates for the batter. • A bat or racket with a bigger surface area to hit the ball promotes higher scoring.

(continued)

TABLE 4.1 *(continued)*

Game modification	Expected outcomes
BASES	
Larger	• Larger boxes increase scoring. • Larger boxes encourage the runner to try to run more often. • Larger boxes make it harder for the defense to cover the boxes.
Smaller	• Smaller boxes increase defensive outs. • Smaller boxes promote offensive players remaining in the box. • Smaller boxes allow for the defense to defend the boxes more easily.
Distance between	• A greater distance promotes less running and increases passing. • A greater distance forces the offensive players to devise more complex tactics for running. • The farther the boxes are apart, the less scoring occurs.
TIME LIMITS	
Limiting the time defensive player can hold the ball	• Passing among defensive players increases. • Runner's opportunities to return to the box improve. • More defensive players are included in game play.
Limiting the time offensive player can stay in the box	• Runners are forced to plan and execute tactics more quickly. • Offensive players take more risks. • The pace of the game increases, but fewer runs are scored.
SCORING	
1 point for returning to the batter's box	• Most difficult for the offense. • Forces offensive players to think through tactics more thoroughly. • Scoring remains low. • Harder for offensive players who are less skilled.
1 point for successfully running to the safety box and 1 point for returning to the batter's box	• Increases opportunities for less skilled players. • Tactics are influenced by equal importance being placed on safety and batter's box.
1 point for successfully running to the safety box and 2 points for returning to the batter's box	• Less skilled players have more opportunities to score. • Defense protects both safety box and batter's box with greater emphasis on the batter's box.

Adapted, by permission, from J.R. Todorovich, 2008, "A dynamic-rules game for teaching striking-and-fielding game tactics," *Journal of Physical Education, Recreation and Dance* 79(5): 26-33.

Invasion Games

Invasion games are those where a team travels with an object and tries to score by getting it into a goal or over a line. In these games, both teams are concurrently trying to complete the same task. That is, both teams need possession in order to move upfield and score, and accordingly in most invasion games there are rules allowing for players to take possession from an opponent. Table 4.4 shows that these games can be focused on using the hand, foot, or stick as the modality of moving the ball and whether the scoring target is focused (as in a goal) or more open ended (as in scoring over an end line).

TABLE 4.2—Tag Games	
Combative	**Chasing, fleeing, dodging**
Fencing Kendo Boxing Taekwondo	Laser tag

TABLE 4.3—Target Games	
Unopposed (indirect)	**Opposed (direct)**
Bocce Croquet Curling Golf Lawn bowls Shuffleboard Table games (pool, billiards)	10-pin bowling Archery Darts Shooting sports

TABLE 4.4—Invasion Games			
Ball in hand		**Ball on foot**	**Ball on stick**
Focused target	Open-ended target	Focused target	Focused target
Basketball Netball Handball	Frisbee Rugby American football	Australian football Soccer	Hockey Lacrosse Hurling Polo

Striking and Fielding Games

Striking and fielding games are those where a ball is hit and then players have to run from one point to another in order to score. These games are different from invasion and net or wall games in that teams take turns in the offensive and defensive roles. Striking and fielding games are played on either fan-shaped fields (e.g., baseball, softball, rounders), where the ball is always sent forward and must travel within a designated area, or oval-shaped fields, where the ball is normally struck from the center of the playing field and can be hit to all points 360 degrees of the playing area (e.g., cricket, stoolball) (table 4.5 on page 42).

TABLE 4.5—Striking and Fielding Games	
Fan shaped	**Oval shaped**
Baseball Softball Rounders	Cricket Stoolball Vigoro

Net and Wall Games

Net games and wall games are those where the primary goal is to strike an object either over a net or to a wall in such a way that your opponent cannot return it. When playing over a net, some games use either a racket or hand, whereas most wall games are played on a shared space and use a long-handled implement (table 4.6). However, the game of jai alai is one where the ball is not struck but slung from a long scoop. Walleyball is a game that is played over a net but within an enclosed space so that the walls are also in play.

TABLE 4.6—Net and Wall Games			
Net: divided space		**Wall: shared space**	**Net and wall**
Racket	Hand	Racquetball Squash Jai alai	Walleyball
Badminton Tennis Table tennis Pickleball	Volleyball		

Conclusion

No matter the game, it is the rules of that game that give it shape, by describing what players must, can, and cannot do. Changing the rules of any game will change the way it is played, and it is a goal of this book for students to understand the various ways in which rules shape tactics. With that in mind, this chapter has outlined the ways in which various games can be placed in similar categories and offers a starting point for games design.

References

Grehaigne, J.-F., Richard, J.-F., & Griffin, L.L. (2005). *Teaching and learning team sports and games.* New York: RoutledgeFalmer.

Hardman, A., Fox, L., McLaughlin, D., & Zimmerman, K. (1996). On sportsmanship and "running up the score": Issues of incompetence and humiliation. *Journal of the Philosophy of Sport, 23,* 58-69.

Huizinga, J. (1950). *Homo Ludens.* London: Paladin.

Suits, B. (1978). *The grasshopper: Games, life and utopia.* Toronto: University of Toronto Press.

PART II

Designing Basic Games

- Understand the five basic games categories.
- Play sample games for each category.
- Use a template of design questions to guide students in making their own games.

In order to create good games, both students and teachers can benefit from more than a superficial knowledge of how games work. The purpose of part II is to increase your understanding of the various game types so you can give students experiences that allow them to create games that are tactically challenging and engaging. Part II, then, is the main course and provides the bulk of material for this book.

Chapters 5 (tag games), 6 (target games), 7 (invasion games), 8 (striking and fielding games), and 9 (net and wall games) all follow a similar format. First, the game form is described together with its underlying key tactical concepts. Next, the skills and learning experiences required for successful play in these games are outlined. Sample games are also included. You are encouraged to play these games with your students before they begin the design process. In this way, they should develop some tactical awareness as well as an expanded repertoire of experiences they can use when they design their own games. Having students play these sample games and watching their participation in them will also allow you to construct the design brief for students in a way that will maximize their potential for success.

The key strategies common to games in the game type are then introduced. Having a good knowledge of these strategies will allow you to make suggestions and interventions if the game-making process gets stalled. Examples of poor games are also provided to highlight certain game features that make them less attractive. Safety is also addressed.

Finally, each chapter contains a "questions to consider" section that presents games designers with a number of stimulus questions they can think about as they develop their games. A template is also provided that you can copy and give to students that summarizes the different options for playing the particular game form.

CHAPTER 5

Tag Games

ag games are those where the players try to "tag" a certain place on an opponent's body. In some tag games, the tag is made using the hands, as is the case in boxing. In others such as fencing, the tag is made with an implement such as a sword. In paintball, players use compressed-air guns to tag other players with paint-filled pellets. In many tag games the target areas are limited by the rules. For example, in boxing, scores are given for punches that strike the front or sides of the opponent's body (above the belt) or head. In sabre fencing, the target areas are the arms and head.

In play and physical education, we see a different form of tag relationship. Here, there are designated taggers, and the rest of the players are moving to avoid being tagged. Requiring neither teams, nor scores, nor sports equipment such as balls, tag games can easily be made more complex with various rule modifications. Both of these aspects make tag a popular game among children, and it is often played in informal areas such as playgrounds or backyards.

Traditionally, tag games meant anyone who got tagged was out. However, the best tag games give participants a way to get back into the game or provide them with an alternative role until the game is over. Most tag games thus will often involve "untag" options, where someone who is free can release the frozen player. Examples include giving a high five or doing a leap frog over the frozen player, trading places with the tagger, or joining the tagger as a second tagger (or joining the tagger's team). Many tag games include additional rules relating to whether another player is eligible as a target, as well as "no tag-backs," where a player cannot tag the person who has just tagged her. Still other rules can render a player "safe" when he is on or in a predetermined zone (such as a poly spot).

Key Principles of Tag Games

When a boxer follows a jab with a cross or a taekwondo player follows a punch with a kick, these players are using a strategy that tries to overload the opponent. Essentially, they are trying to make the opponent respond to one signal, and while the opponent's brain is responding, they quickly send a second signal. The extra time it takes to respond to the second signal is known as the *psychological refractory period* (PRP). The PRP is like a bottleneck in the brain, as it represents the delay in response to the second of two closely spaced stimuli.

In chasing, fleeing, and dodging games, the PRP is also put in use. Someone running from a chaser may fake a move in one direction and then quickly change to another escape pathway. Skillful chasers may also give out fake cues about where they are headed and then quickly change to another pathway. Likewise, most elite tag players have learned to ignore certain moves from an opponent.

Required Experiences for Success in Tag Games

Participation in tag games can develop movement skills used in many other game forms. Speed and agility are essential for successful participation in most games, and being able to change direction quickly also requires significant *dynamic balance* (balance while the body is moving).

Participation in tag games also helps develop an awareness of direction. To dodge or flee, one often has to move sideways or backward. Furthermore, as most tag games are played within specific boundaries, you need to be aware of the spaces that provide maximum advantage or disadvantage to the player on the attack or defense.

For students to become competent games players, they should have experiences in a number of activities that would be classed in the agility category. Partner movements such as copying and contrasting are good places to begin. The challenge here is to copy or contrast the movement of the partner as quickly as possible. These can be footwork pathways, different body positions, or changes in levels. Trying to "lose your shadow" by changing direction quickly is another useful and fun activity for beginning tag players. We know that the skill progression in moving seems to be easiest for moving forward, more difficult sideways, and most difficult backward.

Practice in faking should also be included in preparation for tag games. Faking includes the skill of making a move in one direction and then quickly changing direction without losing balance or speed. Students can practice faking both individually and with a partner. Faking can also be effected by changes in body position, particularly changes in levels. Partner tag games in a restricted playing area allow the student to focus on just one other person while also thinking about faking and then moving. Large-group tag games may diffuse such focus, especially when these faking skills are first developing.

Photo courtesy of Rafa Puerta. r.lopezdieguezpuerta@gmail.com

Dynamic balance allows one to change direction quickly.

Key Strategies for Success in Tag Games

Tag games can be divided into two broad categories. The first are the combat games such as boxing, fencing, and other martial arts where two contestants face off to try to tag each other (often with weapons). The second category includes all those games based upon chasing, fleeing, and dodging. Although the key strategies for these games will differ depending upon the two categories, the use of the PRP (i.e., giving a fake or using one move to set up another) is common to all tag games. Perhaps the best description of tactics in tag games comes from Charles L. de Beaumont (1952), who claimed that fencing is a game of subtlety, and bluff can be met with counter-bluff.

COMBAT GAMES

Within these one-on-one sports, the main tasks are to try to make a hit while at the same time avoiding being hit.

When attacking, you have three choices. First, you can make a full-out attack trying to score. Alternatively, you can fake an attack one way to put your opponent off guard and then attack from another point. Third, you may show your opponent what she thinks might be an attack opening for her, but as she makes her move (which you have predicted), you then make your strike.

When defending, you also have three choices. The first is to avoid contact by dodging or moving away. If this is not possible, you can block or deflect the attack from your opponent. The third option, rather than taking a defensive position, is to counterattack. These decisions are shown in figure 5.1.

Essentially, these tactics revolve around *timing* and *distance*. That is, the main tactical purpose is to *anticipate or be ahead of* the opponent. First, you have to anticipate the opponent in time, or be a thought ahead of him. A player may take advantage of potentially suitable situations or may actively create situations suitable to his purpose by careful preparatory action.

Second, you must have the ability to be the distance from an opponent that is optimal for you and most difficult for him. For example, it would be a mistake to

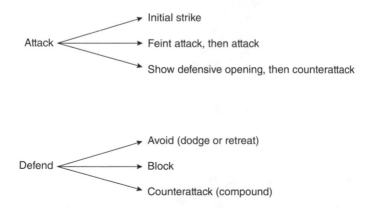

FIGURE 5.1 **Combat game options for attack and defense.**

move in close for an attack when your opponents are concentrated and waiting for an attack. It is far more valuable to close this distance when the opponent is temporarily off balance, not concentrated, or expecting something quite different. Generally speaking, practically all tag fighting actions and the footwork accompanying them aim, in a way, at gaining nearness while preserving combat initiative. However, when attacking, the attack distance must be just right. That is, if after your attack the defender backs up or dodges, you may get caught leaning or overextending to reach for the target. Once you are overextended on the first attack, your time to transition to the next phase or to a new action increases, shifting the initiative to your opponent.

CHASING, FLEEING, AND DODGING GAMES

In chasing, fleeing, and dodging games, Belka (1998, 2006) has outlined four main tactics. These are (1) be balanced at all times, ready to move in any direction; (2) use many kinds of fakes when tagging and when avoiding tags; (3) dodge by changing speed and direction quickly and unexpectedly; and (4) know what is happening in front of you, behind you, and on either side.

- **Being balanced.** The most important skill a tag game player needs to understand and use is how to maintain a balanced, ready position that allows quick movement in a variety of directions. The ready position involves quickly lowering one's weight by bending the knees comfortably, with the feet about shoulder-width apart. Many children mistakenly lean forward from the waist in the ready position. Although this allows them to move forward easily, it makes shifting weight to either side difficult and moving backward an even bigger problem. Of course, many children do not realize that they can move backward to avoid a chaser; that strategy should be part of learning to play tag games, too.

- **Faking.** Knowing how and when to fake is essential in many adult sports and also in tag games. Children can be taught to use various parts of the body to make other players believe they are going to do one thing when they are planning to do another. Using various body parts and, later, one's eyes to fake needs to be practiced in a variety of situations.

- **Changing speed and direction.** Direction and speed of movement are also related to faking. Running at full speed is not always the most effective

Ready to chase or flee.

means of chasing and can lead to running off course when that opponent changes direction quickly. More appropriate is deception. That is, the "it" needs to learn to conceal the direction, speed, and instant she will move in order to confuse the player being chased. And the one being chased needs to use these strategies, too.

- **Being aware of the play space.** An essential skill in tag games is knowing what is happening to your front, sides, and back. Players must be aware of their surroundings. This means they must frequently scan different areas, quickly analyze what is happening, and then decide instantly how and when to move or not to move. Players need also be aware of the spaces on the playing area where they can either trap an opponent or be trapped by a potential tagger. On rectangular courts, these danger spots are usually the corners or along the sidelines and baselines. Although they may be good places to "hang out," you must be ready to move quickly away when danger lurks. It is worthwhile, then, to have students design simple one-on-one, or one-on-two tag games using differently shaped areas such as circles, diamonds, or polygons.

Sample Tag Games

This section will provide examples of various types of tag games. The variations relate mainly to the *method of untagging*. Having students play these simple and quick games should help them to understand the different ways in which tag games can develop.

ANYONE CAN UNFREEZE

In these games, players who are tagged can be unfrozen by any other player. The method of unfreezing is limited only by the imagination.

Ghostbusters

▶ Six to eight students are designated as "slimers." The slimers are to tag their classmates with soft foam balls (the balls are not thrown). When tagged, a student must stop and stand with her legs in straddle position.

▶ To be deslimed, another student must run up and say, "Who ya gonna call?" The person who is slimed must say, "Ghostbusters!" The student who approached the slimed student then slides through the slimed student's legs or gives her a high five, and that person is then free to run again.

Beanbag Tag

▶ One or two players act as chasers to tag the moving players. Two (or more) of the moving players have a beanbag to use as either a "safe" or a "freeing" device. The beanbag can be passed or thrown to other players who are frozen. When a frozen player catches the beanbag, he is free.

▶ Players with beanbags can still be tagged.

SAFE PLAYERS CAN UNFREEZE

In these tag games, designated players cannot be tagged, and they are the only ones who can unfreeze a tagged player. The "safe" players remain in that role until the game ends. Again, the method of unfreezing varies by game.

Jack Frost Tag

▶ One or more students are chosen to be Jack or Jill Frost (i.e., the taggers). They are identified by wearing bright scarves. Two to four other students are the snow angels and carry the hand warmers (yarn balls or beanbags). Anyone Jack or Jill tags becomes a frozen snowman.

▶ To unfreeze the snowman, a snow angel must give him a hand warmer. An unfrozen snowman becomes a snow angel, and the person who gave him the hand warmer can now get tagged. Jack or Jill Frost cannot tag snow angels.

Fire and Ice

▶ Three students have blue balls that represent ice, and two students have red balls that represent fire. Everyone else is free and can run wherever they want.

▶ The ice people try to freeze the free people by tagging them with the blue balls. When students get tagged by an ice person they become frozen (standing still with both hands on head). The fire people (who can't be tagged by the ice people) try to free all of their frozen teammates, by handing them a red ball.

▶ The fireballs keep getting passed on and on, but the ice people stay ice people until the game ends.

Sharks, Seals, and Dolphins

▶ Three students are the sharks, and each shark has a small Gator Skin ball. Three students are dolphins, and each has a scooter. The rest of the class are seals. Two unfolded mats are placed on each side of the gym. The mats represent islands, which are safe zones from the sharks. The gym floor represents the ocean.

▶ Only the seals may go on the islands, and they can stay there for only five seconds before they have to leave. They also may not leave a mat and get right back on the same mat. Sharks may not stand and wait in front of the islands.

▶ When a seal gets tagged, she must lie down and wait for a dolphin to come rescue her. The dolphin will scoot over to the seal that is lying down, and they will switch places. The dolphin will push the seal on the scooter to the closest island, where the seal will stand up and is back in the game. Seals that are being rescued are to sit on the scooter as well.

▶ Sharks can't tag the dolphins or the seals that are being rescued.

Everybody's It

▶ In this game everyone has the power to tag everyone else and is in the game until tagged four times.

▶ As people are tagged, they lose the ability to use appendages. The first tag, they lose use of one arm. The second tag, they lose the ability to use both arms and can no longer tag. The third tag, they can hop on one foot. The fourth tag, they are out of this round and kneel down.

▶ Two people are selected as ambulances. The ambulances run around making siren sounds and tag kneeling students on the head. When tagged on the head by an ambulance, the students' arms and legs are healed, and they are free to run around again.

MULTIPLE-OPTION TAGGERS

In these games there are multiple taggers, but each group of taggers has limits on what they can do. Unfreezing is usually the job of a set of designated players, but of course, the end product will be determined by those designing the game.

Jurassic Park Tag

▶ Choose one person to be the Tyrannosaurus rex, and give that person a red Nerf ball. This dinosaur eats meat but has bad eyesight. If a player is standing still, she cannot be tagged by the T. rex. This dinosaur may only tag his prey.

▶ Choose one person to be a Diloposaurus. This dinosaur spits! Give this dinosaur a different-colored ball. She may throw the ball and hit a player below the shoulders. This dinosaur has good eyesight, so she can also get prey that is standing still.

▶ Choose two people and give them each a colored ball different from the others. These are the Velociraptors. They hunt in twos or in packs. They can only tag their prey together at the same time. They eventually (especially the older ones) figure out that they have to corner their prey or follow the T. rex around and wait for his prey to stand still. A player who is tagged by any meat-eating dinosaur sits down.

▶ Choose two people and give them each a scooter board. They are the Brontosauruses, which are plant-eating dinosaurs. They do not eat the people and will unfreeze those who have been frozen. The Brontosauruses can't be tagged by the meat-eating dinosaurs.

SAFE ZONES

These are the tag games where players can avoid being tagged when they occupy a designated space. Rules can be introduced about how long players can remain in the space and about what happens if another player wants that space.

Fox and Squirrel

▶ To start out, you have four students stand on poly spots. These are squirrels. You will also have a student stand in the middle of the gym. This is also a squirrel. The remainder of those playing are foxes, who are in a line against the wall or outside the playing area.

▶ The objective of the game is for the first fox in line to tag the squirrel in the center. At any time the squirrel can tag any of the squirrels standing on the poly spots, and they trade places. Now the fox would be chasing a new squirrel. If the squirrel on the dot leaves the dot before being tagged, that person has to go to the back of the fox line.

▶ When the fox tags a squirrel, the squirrel goes to the back of the fox line, and the fox becomes the new squirrel.

Corner Tag

▶ This game is played on one side of a volleyball court. Each corner (there are six in total) is a safe zone.

▶ Players standing on a corner cannot be tagged, but they must vacate the corner if another player wishes to occupy it.

▶ There are usually two taggers. If a player is tagged, then she becomes a tagger, and the tagger becomes a regular player.

▶ Players forced out of bounds also switch with the tagger.

TAG GAME SPORTS

Although the tag games mentioned to date are mostly considered part of the play regime in physical education or during breaks in school, in South Asia there are two tag games that are highly organized and competitive. Kabaddi is the more widespread of the two, being played throughout India, Pakistan, Bangladesh, Sri Lanka, and Iran. Kabaddi has been a medal sport at the Asian Games and even has a world championship. The other tag sport is called kho-kho, and it provides a great example of a sophisticated game that students could play before designing their own games.

In kho-kho, eight members of one team sit or kneel in the middle of the court, alternately facing the opposite direction, while the ninth member is an active chaser and stands at either of the posts, ready to begin the pursuit. The other team sends three members onto the court. The motive for the sitting and chasing team is to try to tag the opponents. A match consists of two innings in which an inning consists of chasing and running turns of 7 minutes each.

Photo courtesy of Arti Sandhu.

Kho-kho is a highly organized and competitive tag game.

Members of the chasing team have to put the opponent out, touching him with their palms but without committing a foul. Defenders have full freedom of movement on both sides of the central lane, but the active chaser cannot cross the central lane, unlike the defenders, who can run randomly and in between the sitters. An active chaser can change position with a seated chaser by touching him from behind with the palm and uttering the word *kho* loudly. The attack is built up through a series of *khos* as the chase continues with a relay of chasers.

All the action in kho-kho is provided by the defenders, who try to play out the seven-minute playing time, and the chasers who try to dismiss them. Defenders enter the playing area in batches of three. After the third and last defender of a batch is out, the next batch must enter the game before a *kho* is given by the successful active chaser. At the end of the innings, there is an interval of five minutes and an interval of two minutes in between the turns. Each side alternates between chasing and defense.

Poor Tag Games

Poorly designed tag games are notorious for two flaws, namely high amounts of waiting and, associated with this, elimination. In particular, line games and circle games are those where there are many participants, but only one or two players are active at any time. Consider the following example, which closely resembles duck, duck, goose.

Choose one player to be the runner and one player to be the chaser. All other players are to lie in a big circle in groups of two. The players lie side by side on their bellies, their heads facing the center of the circle. There is a space between each group of two players. On go, the chaser will try to tag the runner. The runner will run on the outside of the circle and try to find a space to lie down next to one set of players. The player on the opposite side of that pair will have to get up and start running from the chaser. If the runner is tagged, then she is to turn around and chase the chaser. The new runner will find a spot to lie down, and the player on the opposite side will start running because he is the new runner.

Here is a game with only two active participants, and the rest of the players are not only inactive but also not learning anything about tag strategies. Along with its cousin, duck, duck, goose, this game certainly earns its entry into the Hall of Shame.

If you do a quick review of the sample games presented earlier in this chapter, you will note that none of them involved players being eliminated when they were tagged. That is, in none of the games did we see a situation exist where as players are tagged, they are out and have to wait until the game is finished to reenter. There were always other options such as becoming a tagger or being unfrozen.

Elimination makes no sense from a pedagogical perspective, as those often caught first are the ones who are lacking in the skills and movement abilities that these games are meant to develop. Elimination, then, is counterproductive. Although it is unlikely that games designers will include elimination in their games, it is still the responsibility of the teacher to help students discover other options that allow their games to work better.

Although success in tag games favors those who are speedy and agile, it is important for games designers to avoid having the situation arise where one tagger is "it" for too long and can never get out of that role. This discourages and frustrates the chaser, and the other participants will more than likely get bored. An easy fix for this situation is to have the games designers think of either including more taggers or having them explore the boundaries of the game itself.

Safety in Tag Games

There are three key elements of tag games that need to be considered when we think of safety. These are, in order, the *playing space* of the game itself, followed by issues of *how to tag* and then *where to tag*.

PLAYING SPACE

In terms of the space, tag games involve a lot of running and changes of direction. Frequently, the player being chased will be running in among other people, and the potential for collisions is high. It is particularly important for games makers to experiment with the boundaries they are using when playing tag games. It is worthwhile to change the size of the court or field, making it smaller or larger. In addition to the size of the court, its dimensions can also be explored. There are no rules that say tag games have to be played in any specific geometric format, such as a square or rectangle. Using an octagonal shape or perhaps something like a star may enhance a game. This provides more corners and spaces that games designers can designate as safety or specialist zones.

In conjunction with boundaries, another safety consideration is the safety base. In many games there may be segments of the court or spaces where players cannot be tagged when they occupy that space. You must be cautious that those safe places are stable and also won't cause an obstacle that can be run into. Poly spots are useful, though not often large enough. This is remedied by using hoops, but these have tendencies to slide on contact and should be taped down. Players who step on a hoop while running at speed can take a nasty tumble. Securing hoops to the floor with tape helps to keep them in place and also keeps them in the same place. As an aside, it should be noted that in some games, there might be "floating" safe bases, where hoops or poly spots may be passed between teammates.

Designers of tag games also need to determine what would be considered a safe number of players for their game. What is equally important with space and numbers is that the area outside the playing area be free from obstacles. In many tag games, play is on the periphery of the court as players try to use all the available space.

HOW TO TAG

In most backyard tag games, players will tag each other with their hands. You must make sure that this is done in a sensible and safe manner, and in the determination of rules, the strength of the tag must be taken into account. We must also remember that in many tag situations the tag may be from behind. Teams must be cautious that this tag does not involve pushing or shoving.

Tagging is not always with the hands, however. Other common options include using a beanbag, scarf, or flag belt (the tag is made by stealing a flag from the belt). Flag belts are available in two versions. In one case, the entire belt comes off when pulled, while in the second, an individual flag pops out when it is pulled.

Irrespective of the brand, when wearing flags, one of the challenges for rules makers lies in that offensive players can become rough in attempting to grab a player in order to steal a flag. The defensive player may also have a tendency to become overly physical in an attempt not to have a flag stolen. Likewise, if we are using an implement to tag, such as a noodle, we have found that using shorter noodles (e.g., by cutting them in half or in thirds) and using only an upswing rather than a downswing strike allows for less total velocity. If we are using a ball as the tagging object, players need to determine whether the tagger must tag the opponent with the ball. Players will decide what is age relevant for them in terms of doing this in a safe manner. Remember, good games are always inclusive. In any case, as noted before, games designers need to be aware of introducing fouls for hitting too hard and acting in an overly aggressive manner.

WHERE TO TAG

In terms of where to tag, it should be noted that the head and groin should always be off limits, irrespective of the tagging method. Many games use below-the-waist-only tag rules, but essentially, the question of where to tag safely relates to how to tag.

Questions to Consider When Designing Tag Games

Although tag games are relatively simple in terms of equipment and rules, simply asking students to "make up a tag game" can still leave them with insufficient resources to create a quality activity. This section lists the questions that need to be answered by games makers when they create a tag game.

- **What is the format of the game?** The first challenge for tag games designers is to establish the format of the game. Will the game have continuous chasing, dodging, and fleeing as its goal, or will play be more of the combative player-versus-player format?

- **What is the goal of the game?** Once the game format is decided, next the players need to establish the goal of play. Will the challenge be to get to a specific target point without getting tagged (e.g., other side of the court for chasing games, or tagging a certain place on the opponent), or will the goal be to accrue the minimum number of tags in a specific time, or perhaps to be the last player tagged?

- **What are the limits of play?** The purpose of the game will have implications for the space in which the game is played. Space will involve decisions about boundaries, the shape of the court, and the size of the court. Rules will also have to be developed that deal with penalties for moving out of bounds. Safety issues will also be addressed at this point.

● **How many players will be involved?** Although most combat games are two-player games, there are no hard and fast rules about the participation numbers for chasing and fleeing games. For team games, it is usual to have even numbers, but other tag games may not be so limited. What is critical is to have the best playing number to maximize participation, strategy, and fun. Questions to be addressed here include not only the total number of players but also, within games, the total number of taggers. A further differentiation could involve decisions about whether tagging players have special privileges or restrictions (see Jurassic Park tag as an example).

● **How are players allowed to move?** Although most chasing and fleeing games involve fast running, it is possible for games designers to use other forms of locomotion. If space is limited, games can be restricted to fast walking. In the pool, both running and swimming are options. Other tag games might use scooters in some capacity, as Jurassic Park tag does for how the players can unfreeze teammates.

It is not uncommon, however, to read tag game rules where "use various locomotor skills such as skipping or galloping" is given as variation options. Nonetheless, any teacher who has tried these options has quickly discovered that within minutes, absorbed by the excitement of the game, fast walking and running become the norm. The time stress involved in chasing, fleeing, and dodging does not accommodate alternate locomotor skills very well, and it is advised in this text to forgo them.

● **How can you tag someone?** Although tag games have to involve some form of touching or tagging, there are four general categories of tagging that can be explored when designing tag games. The first is simply using the hand to tag. Most teachers will require an open hand or a two-finger tag for safety, while games designers might require a two-hand tag to make life more difficult for the chasers. Rather than using the hand itself, many tag games will involve tagging with an object in the hand. These might include a yarn ball, a scarf, a beanbag, or, as an extension of the hand, a noodle. Third, tagging may be in the form of hitting the fleeing player with a ball. Done in a safe way (teachers and students can explore rules), this form of tagging allows not only for an extended range of tagging but also for the tagging object to be moved among the defending players. Finally, tag belts might be used in cases where it is critical that a tagged player be identified.

● **How can players be unfrozen?** As discussed earlier, most contemporary tag games do not involve elimination. Consequently, games designers need to find ways to include those who have been tagged. Depending upon the goal of the game and the tactics involved, these might include being frozen until unfrozen, exchanging places with the tagger, becoming part of the tagger's team, or returning to one's end zone or a jail (where the player is released by a teammate).

In tag games where scores are kept, players may lose points if they are tagged (e.g., if their flag is stolen). When designing games involving the taking of flags, players may also wish to incorporate ways for those tagged to reload the flag belt. Usually, this is done in a way where the player has to leave the field or court, with the result that the team is now compromised in terms of numbers. When using more than one flag on a belt, the decision becomes whether to reload after one flag loss or to wait and suffer perhaps more harsh consequences if both (or all) flags are taken.

- **Will there be any safety zones?** In many tag games, players are safe if they are located in certain places on the court or field. Safe spaces can include certain lines, corners, or other specific zones designated within the rules. Poly spots, mats, or hoops may also be used. The advantage of these more movable objects is that each team might be given the opportunity to place its own safety bases in locations at their discretion.

Rather than having safe places, some tag games allow players to perform specific actions to remain safe. For example, being in an inverted position (i.e., where the hips are above the head) can make a player safe from tagging. Alternatively, two players who are linked at the elbows might also be safe. No matter what form of safety is incorporated into tag games, games designers will need to determine how long a player is allowed to remain in the safe situation.

A Template for Designing Tag Games

Table 5.1 on page 58 provides a template of decisions that can be given to games makers when they are about to design a target game. Let's consider a sample game that was designed using these key questions.

Cheetah tag is described as an action-packed activity that combines environmental issues with animal rights, spatial awareness (general and personal space), and cardiovascular endurance. It was designed by students at Northside Elementary School in Ann Arbor, Michigan. The rules for cheetah tag are presented in table 5.2 on page 59 using the template for tag game design.

TABLE 5.1—Template for Designing Tag Games	
Design question	**Options**
What is the format of the game?	Chase, flee, dodge One-on-one combat
What is the goal of the game?	Chase, flee, dodge • Get to a specific target point (e.g., other side of the court) • Minimal tags in a time limit • Be the last tagged One-on-one combat • Record more tags on the opponent in the time limit • Be first to record a set number of tags • Be first to tag the critical area
What are the limits of play?	Boundaries or no boundaries? Shape of the court (square, rectangle, circle, polygon) Size of the court Out-of-bounds space
How many players will be involved?	Number of total players Number of taggers Specialist tag roles
How are players allowed to move?	Fast walking Running Swimming Skating Scooter
How can you tag someone?	Hands Beanbag Scarf Noodle Ball (tagged or thrown) Stolen belt flag
How can players be unfrozen?	Freeze until unfrozen Exchange with tagger Become part of tagging team Lose points Return to the beginning point Eliminated (not recommended)
Will there be any safety zones?	On lines On corners On poly spots or mats In hoops In specific court zones When performing specific action (e.g., a specific balance) Time allowed in safety zone

From P. Hastie, 2010, *Student-Designed Games: Strategies for Creativity, Cooperation, and Skill Development* (Champaign, IL: Human Kinetics).

TABLE 5.2—Cheetah Tag

Design question	Options
What is the format of the game?	This tag game is a chasing, fleeing, and dodging game, complete with freeze and unfreeze options, safety bases, and diverse roles for players.
What is the goal of the game?	There are multiple goals for the game depending upon the player's role. First, the cheetahs are trying not to be tagged by the poachers (3 students wearing orange vests). Second, the poachers are trying to avoid being tagged by the conservation officer (1 student wearing a blue vest). Third, the veterinarians (2 students wearing red vests) are trying to rescue injured cheetahs. The game ends when all 3 poachers are captured by the conservation officer or all of the cheetahs are captured by the poachers.
What are the limits of play?	There are no boundaries per se for this game. Sufficient space needs to be provided for a large number of participants.
How many players will be involved?	A minimum of 10 players makes the game work, but a large number can easily be accommodated.
How are players allowed to move?	All players are allowed to run.
How can you tag someone?	Tags are light and made with an open hand.
How can players be unfrozen?	If a poacher (orange vest) tags a cheetah, the cheetah becomes injured (in Northside physical education class, we don't kill or do violent things) and has to sit down where she was tagged to await rescue by a kindly veterinarian (student in red vest). If a poacher is tagged by a conservation officer, the poacher must sit where he was tagged until rescued by another poacher (poacher tags him lightly to unfreeze him).
Will there be any safety zones?	There are three watering holes (hoops), scattered about randomly, and three grazing areas (poly spots), also scattered about randomly, where cheetahs may stand and be safe for 10 seconds.

Conclusion

This chapter has introduced you to two types of tag games: those in which two players engage in some type of combative test, and those that involve participants in the skills of chasing, fleeing, and dodging. All these games can improve participants' dynamic balance and motor skills, and when properly designed to avoid elimination, they can be a source of high-intensity health-enhancing activity.

References

Belka, D.E. (1998). Strategies for teaching tag games. *Journal of Physical Education, Recreation & Dance, 69* (8), 40-44.

Belka, D. (2006). What do tag games teach? *Teaching Elementary Physical Education, 17* (3), 35-36.

de Beaumont, C. L. (1952). *Know the game: Fencing.* London: Amateur Fencing Association/ Educational Productions Ltd.

CHAPTER 6

Target Games

I f you have ever gone bowling or if you have played pool or darts with friends, you have played games belonging to the target games category. Target games are those where a player releases an object in order to hit a specific target. We call it a *release* in target games, in contrast to a throw, because there are many ways of sending the object to the target. Table 6.1 gives some examples of the different implements and releases used in some target games.

Target games not only vary with implement and release mechanism but also differ in terms of whether the player or the target is moving or still. In both darts and bowling, the target is still; but you stand in a designated place when playing darts, while in bowling you walk with the ball to deliver it. Other games and sports involve moving targets. In clay target shooting, shooters are presented with a wide variety of targets that duplicate the flight path of gamebirds. In laser tag and paintball, members from both teams are both shooters *and* targets who move throughout the field of play.

Winning players in target games are usually those who either hit the most targets or get closest to the designated target, but there are other ways to win as well, as seen in table 6.2 on page 62.

TABLE 6.1—Implements and Release Methods in Target Games

Game	Implement	Release
Darts	Dart	Overhand throw
Lawn bowls	Ball that travels on a curved path because of a weight bias	Underhand roll
Golf	Small ball	Struck with a club
Archery	Arrow	Released from a bow
Pool/Billiards	Ball	Struck with a long stick
Curling	Curling stone (circular granite rock)	Pushed
Marbles	Small glass ball	Flicked with fingers
Shooting	Bullet	Shot from a gun or pistol

TABLE 6.2—Scoring Methods in Target Games	
How to win	**Game**
Get the most points by hitting the targets with the highest value	Darts Billiards Archery Shooting
Hit the most targets	10-pin bowling Laser tag Rapid-fire pistol shooting
Be the closest to the target	Lawn bowls Curling Boules sports (including bocce and pétanque) Horseshoes
Be the first to remove, knock down, or progress through all the targets	Pool Croquet
Take the fewest turns to hit all targets (i.e., have the lowest score)	Golf Frisbee golf

You can also differentiate target games by the degree to which you can obstruct your opponent from the target. This is not the *physical* obstruction we think about such as defending in basketball or football, but there are situations in target games where you can keep your opponent from hitting the target. Typically you do this by placing your own object in the pathway needed by your opponent. Think of golf or darts. In these games the actions of your opponents have *no* impact on your ability to hit your target. In pool, snooker, lawn bowls, and curling, however, both players (or teams) share the target space and will often try to obstruct each other by occupying key spaces.

Key Principles of Target Games

Irrespective of their scoring methods, the levels of obstruction, or the equipment used, all target games follow three common principles. The first is that target games, in the main, involve what we call *closed skills*. Motor skills can be described as lying on a continuum ranging from open to closed (see figure 6.1).

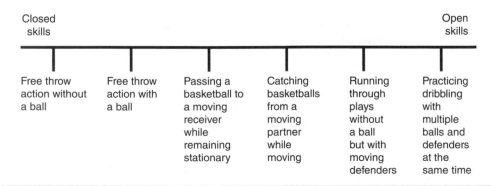

FIGURE 6.1 **Continuum of closed and open skills.**

The open end of the continuum has skills where the environment is unpredictable, whereas the closed end of the continuum has skills where the environment is either stable or predictable as a result of practice. For open skills the environment is constantly changing, which precludes the performer from effectively planning the response. Success seems to be determined by the extent to which the performer can adapt his behavior to the changing environment. In closed skills the environment is much more stable.

The second principle of target games is that *precision and control* are critical for success. Targets are often very small, and your actions have to be almost perfect to be successful. Consider how precise you have to be to hit the bull's-eye in darts, or the control needed to execute a kiss on the pool ball to roll it into the pocket and leave the cue ball in position for the next shot.

Coupled with this idea of small targets is that small errors can be really costly. Olympic gold medals are won by the narrowest of margins (fractions of an inch), and the difference between being the Masters champion in golf or the runner-up could be a putt that lipped out. As an example, in the men's individual gold-medal match of the archery competition at the Beijing Olympics, both Park Kyung-Mo and Viktor Ruban scored 9s and 10s until the 11th round, when Park missed the 9 ring by less than half an inch, scoring an 8. This was the difference between Olympic gold and silver.

The third principle of target games is that they are *self-paced*. By self-paced we mean that you the player decide when to start the action. In throwing a dart or a horseshoe, or in striking a pool ball, you can take your time, take your aim, and shoot when you are ready. Given the need for this precision, concentration, and self-pacing, in most target games spectators are expected to be silent until after the player makes a shot.

Photo courtesy of Mark Walley.

Target games, while self-paced, require great concentration. Small errors can be costly.

Required Experiences for Success in Target Games

Success in target games is dependent upon three motor functions. These are (1) controlling one's force production, (2) controlling one's speed, and, for games where the target is moving, (3) being able to focus quickly on the target. Although some may believe that the best method of attack in bowling is to throw the ball as hard and as fast as possible, being smooth and being able to guide the ball are more productive. Likewise, in games on the pool table, some shots require the most delicate of touches, while others need a firm strike on the cue ball.

Rescue the princess is a good game for demonstrating the importance of, and practicing, controlling force and speed. In this game, four players are trying to rescue a princess from the dragons by knocking over those dragons (with beanbags) without harming the princess herself. This requires manipulating force and speed so that they are sufficient to knock down the dragons, but not so strong as to also knock over the princess's castle. Concurrently, the beanbags must be sent with sufficient force that they will make it out of the circle if they miss a dragon or after they have hit one. Players are restricted by the moat and cannot enter the play area. A beanbag that remains in the circles cannot be retrieved.

Rescue the Princess

PLAYERS

4 players per side

EQUIPMENT

8 beanbags and 10 foam blocks (or 8 balls and 10 wooden blocks), 2 yarn balls

ORGANIZATION

Set up two concentric circles using poly spots or floor tape. In the center circle, place a block with a yarn ball placed on top. This represents the princess on her tower who needs to be saved. The defensive team can then place four more blocks anywhere in this circle to guard the princess. These represent the dragons that are on the island to keep the princess from escaping.

RULES

- ▶ In order to save the princess, players must knock down the opponent's four blocks (dragons), using a beanbag, and *then* knock down the princess's tower and catch her before she hits the ground.
- ▶ Players shoot at the dragons only from outside the outer circle, but they may move around the circle and take their shots from any position.
- ▶ Players cannot enter the outer circle (the moat) to retrieve a beanbag but may use beanbags that travel outside.
- ▶ Once the four dragons are slain, players are free to enter the island to catch the princess as she jumps out of the tower.
- ▶ The first team to defeat all the dragons and save the princess wins.
- ▶ If a team knocks over the princess's tower before all the dragons are slain, the team loses (because she will get burned by the dragons).
- ▶ Two teams compete against each other, playing on the circle set up by their opponent.

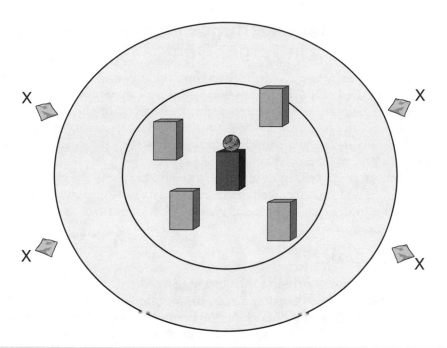

Setup for rescue the princess.

VARIATION

Depending upon the objective, a time limit can be set for saving the princess. This can give students experience at quickly focusing on a target. In this way a player who retrieves a beanbag coming out of the circle must first gather it and then quickly focus on the target dragon. Taking too much time will allow the opposition team to have more throws.

Key Strategies for Success in Target Games

Given they involve mostly closed skills, target games are not as sophisticated in terms of complex strategies when compared with others such as those in the invasion, net and wall, and striking and fielding families. Think about the decisions you make as a batter in softball or baseball. As the pitch is delivered, you first have to decide whether to swing or not, and if you do swing, the focus is then placed on where to hit the ball and with how much power. If you have possession of the ball in basketball or soccer, where the playing environment is constantly changing, you need to decide whether to dribble, shoot, or pass. Both the softball and basketball examples require split-second decision making in the face of the opponent.

The tactics of target games are more about decisions made *before* the action. In golf, there are decisions about club selection, the strength of the swing, and the landing spot. In darts, the decision is about where to aim on the board, and in pool, the decision relates to which ball to hit and which pocket to aim toward. However, in all cases, you determine the initiation of the movement.

Sample Target Games

One of the beauties of target games is that they can be practiced individually, and indeed, elite performers in golf, darts, and table games spend hundreds of hours mastering their skills. Although these athletes can earn millions of dollars from their expertise, in many cultures, the very survival of children and adults often depends on the physical development, skill development, and teamwork learned while playing target games. It is through these target games that children hone their athletic and hunting skills.

In this section, some examples of these indigenous games are given, together with suitable adaptations for their inclusion in physical education. Following these, a series of individual-practice target games is presented, as well as games that are more competitive.

INDIGENOUS GAMES

Many indigenous games relate to the getting of food and as a means of protection against attacks of hostile nationalities. In the games, the targets traditionally represent the hunted, and so many games involve moving targets. The key to success, as in all target games, relates to accuracy, with small errors being costly. Competition winners are usually those who can hit the most targets or who can land their objects most accurately.

Gorri, or Wungoolay

ORIGIN

Australian Aboriginal game

CULTURAL PURPOSE

Learning accuracy of the eye and speed in casting the spear

RULES

A game where Aboriginal boys and men throw or roll a small object along a line at a moving target. Players are required to try to strike the moving object with spears from a distance of about 15 yards (13.7 m) to score points for their team.

ADAPTATIONS

Use a tennis ball as the rolling object, and then throw a weighted noodle as the spear. A weighted noodle is a foam pool noodle with a piece of wooden dowel inserted in the hollow center to provide some rigidity. You can decide whether or not to have a point that can be taped.

Wilkins, 2002

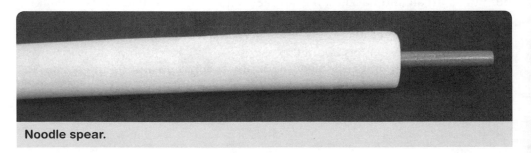

Noodle spear.

Kee'an

ORIGIN

Australian Aboriginal game

CULTURAL PURPOSE

Preparation for hunting and fishing

RULES

A game where competitors throw a large animal bone with twine attached to it over a net into a pit or hole. The goal is that the bone and twine do not touch the net, which requires great skill.

ADAPTATIONS

Toss a beanbag tied to a string over a badminton net and into a hoop on the other side. Again, the aim is to be closest without hitting the net.

Edwards, 1994

Chunkey

ORIGIN

Ho-Chunk, Hidatsa, and Mandan Nation of Wisconsin and Illinois

CULTURAL PURPOSE

Preparation for fishing

RULES

In this game a large stone is rolled over the ground or ice while several players throw spears in an attempt to indicate where the stone will stop rolling. The one closest to the final location of the stone, without actually hitting the stone, is the winner.

ADAPTATIONS

Use a medium-sized ball as the stone and a weighted noodle as the javelin.

Pauketat, 2004

Lasso Throw

ORIGIN

Khanty People of North-Western Siberia

CULTURAL PURPOSE

Preparation for reindeer hunting

RULES

This series of games involves throwing a lasso over a long pole, then a sitting person, then running players (all representing deer). Scoring is by who makes the most accurate throw.

ADAPTATIONS

Place a series of cones at various targets, and toss a deck tennis ring tied to a piece of string.

Krasil'nikov & Sinelnikov, 2006

INDIVIDUAL-PRACTICE TARGET GAMES

The series of tasks that follows can be played alone, where the competition is against oneself, or against a partner. All involve tossing a ball either to a wall or a hoop, and the challenge is simply to increase the distance from the target while repeating the same task. For each success, you move back from the wall one step. For each miss, you move in one step. The challenge is to see how far back you can be after 10 attempts.

- **Wall target.** Toss a ball underhand to the wall into a designated target (e.g., a taped square or a hoop).
- **Wall bounce target.** Throw a ball overhand to bounce once off the floor and into a target on the wall.
- **Hoop floor target.** Toss a ball underhand to land in a hoop on the floor.
- **Wall to hoop target.** Throw a ball overhand to bounce off the wall and then bounce once and land in a hoop on the floor.
- **Two hoops.** Toss a ball underhand to bounce once in the first hoop and then into the second (a progression here is to have the hoops farther apart and have the ball bounce three times—once in the first, once between, and then once in the second hoop).

COMPETITIVE GAMES

The games that follow are more competitive than those listed in the previous section. They are usually played by teams or in pairs, with specific scoring rules included.

Frantic Bowling

In this game, students are in teams of two. In each team, one student is the bowler and the other is the retriever. The bowler bowls, trying to hit an object in the designated area; the retriever runs to pick up the ball, and if an object was hit, brings it back. Play continues for 30 seconds, after which the total number of objects retrieved is the score, and players switch roles.

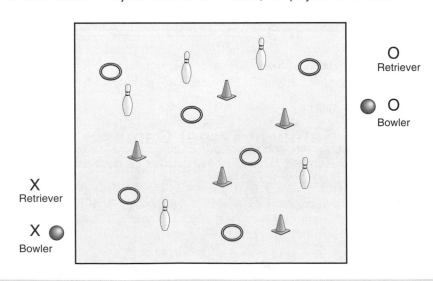

Setup for frantic bowling.

Hillbilly Golf

Hillbilly golf is a good example of a target game with multiple scoring options. The game is played by throwing a bolo of two golf balls connected with a rope at a ladder. Different rungs of the ladder are worth different point values. In most forms of the game, the top rung is worth 3, middle is 2, and bottom is 1.

The goal of the game is to get exactly (and not over) 21 points. In some games, if a player scores over 21, she either reverts to her previous total or goes down that number of points. Depending on house rules, if both teams score on the same rung, those points do not count, or if balls are looped around other balls, those do not count. Other rule sets allow points in both instances.

Playing hillbilly golf.

Photo courtesy of Shana Hancock.

Poor Target Games

By their very nature as self-paced, coupled with safety concerns relating to the firing lines, there is the potential for many target games to involve a lot of waiting time. When designing games, games makers should be encouraged to look for ways in which many players can be active at the same time. This is usually best achieved by having multiple games being played concurrently.

The other feature of target games that adds to nonplaying time is the retrieval factor. In archery, time is spent going from the shooting line to the targets, removing arrows (and sometimes searching for ones that missed), and then returning again to the shooting line. Many target games overcome the retrieval problem by playing in "ends." Horseshoes, the boules sports, and lawn bowls all play in alternate directions, where first you throw to one end of the court and then play again in the return direction.

Safety in Target Games

Safety in target games relates specifically to the shooting and the retrieval parts of the games. Many target games involve sharp objects such as darts or arrows, or even heavy balls, and sometimes these are traveling at speed. The National Rifle Association lists three fundamental rules for safe gun handling that can be used as a good template for safety in target games. These are (1) always point the muzzle in a safe direction; never point a firearm at anyone or anything you don't want to shoot; (2) keep your finger off the trigger and outside the trigger guard until you are ready to shoot; and (3) keep the action open and the gun unloaded until you are ready to use it.

In addition to these handling rules, the key in target games is to make sure the game is designed so there is a clear path between the object and the target. This is achieved by having an established firing line and positioning all students not involved in shooting well behind this line and away from those on the line. In addition, only those on the shooting line should have their implements loaded.

The other issue in target games relates to the collection. First, there needs to be an established starting and stopping procedure for shooting and retrieving. Second, all players need to know how to properly remove their game objects from targets.

Questions to Consider When Designing Target Games

This section lists the questions that need to be answered by games makers when they create a target game.

● **What is the target, and where is it located?** The first decision to be made in a target game is to determine the construction and location of the target. Three key questions need to be answered at this point. All of course can be manipulated with experimentation, but sometimes the equipment that is available is a limiting factor. The first question is "What is the distance to the target?" Players need to decide how far they will be from the target at the point of release. A second and closely related question is "What is the size of the target?" Targets at a greater distance are more likely to be bigger, while nearby targets can be smaller.

The third question is "Where is the target placed?" Is the target on the ground or on a wall? Or is it supported off the ground on a stand or hanging? In addition to its location, the other variable in target location is its angle. A target can be lying flat on the ground or it can be standing up. Likewise, an elevated target such as a hoop can be facing horizontally or vertically. The placement of targets significantly affects the skills used in games. The diagram on page 71 shows some possibilities for target configurations.

● **Is the target moving or still?** Once the target location is determined, you need to decide if the target will be moving or still. Hanging targets often will swing, and hoops and balls acting as targets can easily be rolled. It is important also to decide whether the player shooting at the target is moving or still.

● **What will be used to hit the target?** The next challenge is to decide what will be used as the "sending" object. Will it be a ball that can roll after landing, or a heavier nonbouncing object such as a beanbag or a horseshoe that travels less after landing? Players will then need to determine how that object is to be sent to the target. Will it be an overhand or underhand throw? Will the object be hit, and if that is the case, what will be used to hit or push it? Is there some way the object can be sent other than throwing? Although it is unlikely that students in games making will be using bows and arrows, there are ways to use objects such as a scoop to sling something toward a target.

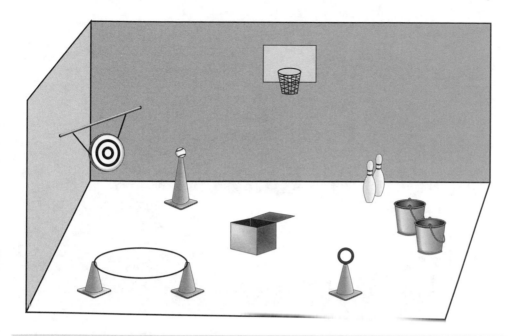

Sample target configurations.

• **What is the goal of the game?** Once the mechanics of the equipment have been decided upon, the next challenge is to determine the goal of the game. As noted earlier in this chapter, winning can be achieved in many different ways. Will winning be achieved by those who hit the most targets or those who get the most points by hitting the targets with the highest value? Alternatively, will the winner be the player who is the closest to the target or who takes the fewest turns to hit all the targets? In some target games the goal may be to progress through a series of targets, with the first one to finish the winner. Games such as pool and croquet are two good examples.

• **What is the scoring system?** Depending upon the goal of the game, games designers will then need to examine how they are going to score. In "hit the most targets," "closest to the target," or "get the most points" games, the key question will be how many throws or turns does the player get to do this. In "getting the highest points" games, the players will need to experiment with different scoring values on their target and decide whether this will be one ringed target or multiple targets with different point values. Finally, for "finish the course" or "take the fewest turns" target games, the decisions will be about how many targets there are to be conquered.

• **Can you hinder your opponent?** In some target games such as those in the boules family and table games such as snooker and pool, players are able to move their opponent's balls to unfavorable positions. Likewise, they are able to place their equipment in order to set up a defense for themselves. When designing a target game, players will need to decide whether there can be any forms of hindrance.

Photo courtesy of Dan Sorensen.

In curling, you can place your rock to block an opponent's access to the center ring.

A Template for Designing Target Games

Table 6.3 provides a template of decisions that can be given to games makers when they are about to design a target game. In table 6.4 on page 74, the game of scooter biathlon is presented using the key design questions.

Biathlon is a term used to describe any sporting event made up of two disciplines. The most common form is the winter sport that combines cross-country skiing and rifle shooting. A biathlon competition consists of a race in which contestants ski around a cross-country track, but after each lap, they must stop and shoot at targets. Either a time penalty or penalty laps are assessed for missed shots. As in most races, the contestant with the shortest total time wins.

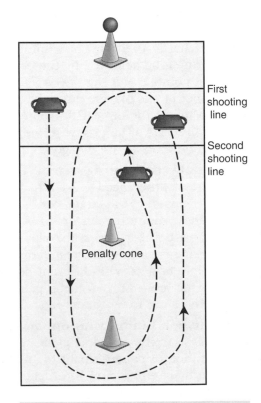

First shooting line

Second shooting line

Penalty cone

Setup for scooter biathlon.

Biathlon combines the most physically demanding sport of cross-country skiing with the intense precision of rifle marksmanship. These opposing disciplines collide at the shooting range. With their hearts pounding nearly three times a second, the athletes struggle to control their breathing as they shoot, knowing that, depending on their shooting performance, extra distance or time is added to their total running distance or time.

For scooter biathlon, you can use scooter boards to simulate the skiing (fitness) component and beanbags for the accuracy component. Alternatively, students can run instead of ride the scooters.

TABLE 6.3—Template for Designing Target Games

Design question	Options
Where is the target?	Distance to target Target size Target placement (height, angle)
What player or target movement is involved?	Player still, target still Player still, target moving Player moving, target still Player moving, target moving
What objects are used?	Ball (light, heavy) Weighted object (beanbag, horseshoes, boules)
How is the object sent to the target?	Underhand toss Roll Overhand throw Push Strike Sling Other form of release
What is the goal of the game?	Get the most points by hitting the targets with the highest value Hit the most targets Be the closest to the target Be the first to remove, knock down, or progress through all the targets Take the fewest turns to hit all targets (i.e., have the lowest score)
How do you score?	Single target Multiple targets Ringed target (one target with scoring zones) How many throws
Is there any hindrance involved?	None Occupying the same space

From P. Hastie, 2010, *Student-Designed Games: Strategies for Promoting Creativity, Cooperation, and Skill Development* (Champaign, IL: Human Kinetics).

TABLE 6.4—Scooter Biathlon	
Design question	**Solutions**
Where is the target?	The target in this game is a small hoop mounted on a traffic cone. The hoop is placed 5 ft (1.5 m) from the first shooting line and 10 ft (3 m) from the second shooting line.
What player or target movement is involved?	The target is not moving, nor is the shooter at the time of the shot.
What objects are used?	A beanbag is used as the implement.
How is the object sent to the target?	The scooter rider will throw a beanbag at the target. As long as the beanbag travels through the target, it is considered a success. The beanbag can be tossed in any manner (e.g., underhand or overhand) to the target. The timekeeper will replace the beanbags at the relevant line after the rider has made 5 shots.
What is the goal of the game?	The goal of the game is to take the shortest total time to complete the course.
How do you score?	Students will begin at the first shooting line. They then ride the scooter around the large traffic cone and back to that line. From this point they take 5 shots at the target with the beanbags from a lying position. For each miss, the rider must complete a penalty circuit about the small cone.
	On the second round, the rider travels again on the scooter around the large cone but returns to the second shooting line. Here, the 5 beanbags can be shot from a sitting position. In this case, for each target missed, 10 s are added to the total time.
	Distances for shooting and travel are totally negotiable by the games players, as is the size of the hoop. Penalties for misses are also flexible. In some games, the penalty may only be added time, while in others there may be different penalty laps.
Is there any hindrance involved?	There is no hindrance or obstruction to the players when they are riding or shooting at the target.

Conclusion

At first glance, one gets the idea that target games simply involve throwing something at a stationary target to score points. As you will now be aware, there are a number of different combinations of player and target movement that are possible for students to use when designing target games. Indeed, trying to create moving targets that are functional is one of the most enjoyable challenges when creating a target game.

References

Edwards, K. (1994). Aboriginal games. *Active & Healthy Magazine, 1* (3), 3-4.

Krasil'nikov, V., & Sinelnikov, O. (2006). Northern Russian "People" games for children. *Teaching Elementary Physical Education, 17* (5), 8-12.

Pauketat, T.R. (2004). *Ancient Cahokia and the Mississippians.* Cambridge: Cambridge University Press.

Wilkins, S.E.D. (2002). *Sports and games of medieval cultures.* Westport, CT: Greenwood Press.

CHAPTER 7

Invasion Games

Your goal in this strategy game is to recruit troops and send them to destroy an enemy castle. You must use tactics to decide what troops to have for each level and when to deploy those troops so that they can best attack the castle and be successful in destroying it.

These are the instructions for the www.Online Games-Zone.com game Invasion 4. Consider how we might describe a game of American football.

Your goal is to recruit players and send them to the other end of the field to score a touchdown. You must use tactics to decide which players should run with the ball, which ones receive passes, and which ones block as well as where to send these players on the field to give them the best opportunity to get into the end zone.

Fundamentally, there is not much difference between these two games, and it is the major challenge of invasion games (and essentially the source of fun) to select appropriate actions from a variety of options, generally in a restricted time or space (pressure) situation. It is easy to see where the term *invasion* came from for describing football, basketball, and lacrosse. A team must pool its resources to move some object downfield, "invade" the defending team's goal area, and ultimately score.

Although simple in intent, the constant interplay between attackers and defenders and the strategy involved make invasion games particularly complex. Perhaps Theresa Maxwell said it best when she noted, "The player must select an appropriate skill and tactic, either individually or in combination with teammates, and in response to both individual and team defenses presented by opponents. The complexity is increased by the ability of both offensive and defensive players to occupy any space in the playing area and to actively interfere with offensive initiatives" (Maxwell, 2006, page 58).

Key Principles of Invasion Games

Irrespective of whether they are played indoors, outdoors, with a stick and a ball, on ice, on horseback, or in a swimming pool, all invasion games have three common principles. It is also important to note that these must be achieved in order. They are possession, progression, and scoring.

POSSESSION

As in the days of old when attacking the castle, the forces of invasion must have had some equipment with which they were going to conquer their opponents. So it is the case in contemporary sport that you must have possession of the ball in order to score. If we discount situations where a team accidently scores in its own goal (such as in soccer or hockey), of all the invasion games that exist, there is only one in which you can score without having the ball—and that is the safety in American and Canadian football. Possession, then, is critical, and it is the first task of any team in an invasion game.

PROGRESSION

No matter the game, it is virtually impossible to score from one's own defensive area. We don't see goalkeepers in soccer trying to kick the ball into the opponent's goal, nor do we see shots taken from the defensive free-throw line in basketball. Very rarely in ice hockey will a team score from its defensive zone—usually only in an empty net situation where the opposition team has mustered all its forces in order to score and has left its goal totally unguarded.

Once a team has possession, it must move the ball up the court or field in order to score. Of course, there are almost unlimited ways in which this progression can take place, such as dribbling with the hands, the feet, or a stick; running; or passing from player to player. Notably, however, for each method of progression there are almost as many limitations on how teams can do this.

In rugby games, for example, you can only pass backward, while in American football you lose possession if you don't meet a progression requirement of 10 yards within four attempts. In some games, you are allowed to progress to place your players anywhere on the field. For example, Australian rules football, basketball, and team handball do not have offside rules. However, in rugby, soccer, and hockey there are stipulations that when a team progresses, the players on that team must be in specific positions in relation to the ball or puck or to the opposition. As a result, one of the progression-stopping strategies used by defenses in soccer is called the offside trap. Progression rules have a significant impact on the way teams are able to move the ball and the ways in which they use space. However, the fundamental goal for a team once it has possession is to move toward the goal.

In games such as basketball where rebounding is possible, an offensive rebound renders the progression requirement moot. Whereas a defensive rebound stops an opponent from getting the ball and eliminates the chances of scoring, the offensive rebound cuts out the need to progress all the way up the court in order to score.

SCORING

Although it is not unusual to hear the catchcry that "defense wins championships," it should be remembered that there is not a single invasion game where a team wins by scoring *fewer* points. Offense and scoring, then, are critical to success and cannot be undervalued. Certainly a team's ability to stop its opponents from scoring has a significant influence on the final outcome of the game, but if a team is unable to convert its own possessions into scores, it is doomed to finish on the losing side of the match ledger.

In most invasion games, any player is able to score, provided he satisfies the rules. There are a few games, however, where this is not the case. In netball there are designated shooters and goal assistants, and in American football, the players of the interior offensive line are ineligible receivers and, by consequence, cannot score.

Required Experiences for Success in Invasion Games

No matter the form of an invasion game, they all involve sending and receiving. We use the terms *sending* and *receiving* rather than throwing and catching because they are more inclusive of games such as hockey and lacrosse. Nonetheless, irrespective of the implement used or the type of ball thrown, students need experience in two particular areas of play—passing and shooting.

Although most students understand the need to pass a ball to move it, many may not be aware of the concepts of the *catchable pass* or the *lead pass*. In terms of catchable passes, students need to understand that while one player may easily catch a pass, the same pass may be problematic for a different teammate. That is, the ball needs to be sent with an appropriate force and speed that the particular receiver can handle. In addition, it should be reinforced that some players are skillful at catching on the run, while others will need to be in a more stable and stationary position.

In terms of the lead pass, the idea is that the throw is made ahead of the receiver so the ball and receiver both arrive at the point of catching together. One of the greatest limitations to progression downfield is a throw behind the receiver. Such a pass not only interrupts the flow of the play and the timing of the receiver but also slows down the team's progression. With this is mind, players need to get open to receive a lead pass, and so instruction on cutting and faking is particularly beneficial in the development of quality invasion games players. A strong background in tag games acts as a wonderful preparation for the movement skills required in invasion games.

Throwing a lead pass.

With regard to lead passes and catchable passes, there are eight common errors that can occur when passing or sending the ball:

1. Throwing behind the receiver
2. Throwing too hard
3. Trying to throw lob passes over defenders (passing too high)
4. Holding the ball too long
5. Not seeing the open receiver
6. Passing too soon
7. Passing to well-defended receivers
8. Traveling (running with the ball when this is illegal)

Rovegno et al., 2001

The second set of experiences that players need for competence in invasion games is those that develop shooting skills. We know from our experiences with target games that many of them are self-paced, but in most invasion games, the time in which the goal is open and the player is unguarded is often very short. Although it is important to develop techniques of ball control that allow for good shooting, there also needs to be practice at taking shots under some form of pressure. Practicing shooting using the four stages of defense described later in this chapter is a good progression toward developing competent shooters.

Key Strategies for Success in Invasion Games

From a tactical perspective, invasion games can be divided into offensive and defensive strategies, and these can be examined from a team or an individual angle. In addition, there are specific tactics that come into play during transitions, those times when a team has just gained or just lost possession.

TASKS OF THE OFFENSE

When a team is on offense, its primary objective is to score. In order to do so, it should follow three key principles. These are creating space, creating an overload near the scoring target, and taking high-percentage shots.

When on offense, the team in possession needs to create space by finding open lanes in which to pass, run, or dribble with the ball. The goal here is to put some distance between the player in possession and a defender. If the offensive team has a player or two who can make successful shots from long distance (e.g., a 3-point shooter in basketball or a great wide receiver in American football), this forces the defense to move closer to the ball to stop the shot or progression. This drawing of the defense out from its goal opens up the play for other attacking players who can cut in to be close to the target.

Once a team nears the scoring target, it should try to create an overload so that there are more players in a position to score than there are defenders available to stop them. The challenge is to get the ball to the most open player to take a shot on goal, hopefully against no defender, or at best against only one. The third point is for the attacking team to take high-percentage shots.

From an individual offensive perspective, a player can be in one of three positions. First, she can have possession of the ball. Second, she can be located near one of her teammates who has the ball. Third, she may be somewhere else on the court or field away from the ball. The player in possession should progress through the following sequence of questions. First, "Can I shoot?" If the answer is no, the next question will be "Can I pass to someone who can shoot?" If the answer is again no, the question becomes "Can I dribble or run to improve my chances of achieving one of the first two options?" Of course, in invasion games these questions must be answered in a split second.

If the player does not have the ball but is close to a teammate who does, the first responsibility is to support that player. This could be achieved by moving into a position to receive a pass or by moving into a space that the player in possession can use to advantage in escaping the defender. An example here would be setting a screen.

If an offensive player is away from the ball, his job is to put himself in a position where he may be able to receive the ball with a long pass or to perform some form of move that will draw defending players out of position.

TASKS OF THE DEFENSE

The tasks of the defending team are essentially opposite to those of the offense. They are trying to occupy the key spaces of the high-percentage shots and to deny this space to the attackers. At the same time, some part of the defensive strategy should be to put pressure on the ball. This can deny a shot at goal, reduce or stop progression, or even be a way to gain possession. Although the offensive team is trying to bring the defenders away from the goal, the defensive unit is trying to push the attackers away from the target.

An individual defender will be in one of three situations: (1) the player closest to the ball, (2) a player nearby the ball, or (3) a player at a distance. The first task of the player closest to the ball is to apply pressure on the ball carrier—ultimately with the goal of getting possession. If gaining possession is not possible, the aim becomes to stop or at least delay the movement of the ball.

Does the second defender help the player on the ball or cover space?

The player close to the ball has a series of complex decisions. This player will need to decide whether to help the ball defender and put extra pressure on the ball carrier in a double-team situation or to remain off the ball but pick up the player who would be the target of the player in possession. Another decision may be to move into the space that is the likely route of the ball carrier if she beats her defender. Finally, the best option may be to retreat toward the goal.

The players farthest from the ball will take a similar role to the second player, but without pressuring the ball. They will need to decide if they should move into the eventual pathway of the ball carrier or someone who is more likely to receive, or not to worry about the ball but to cover other players who are moving toward the goal.

TASKS ON TRANSITION

If on a transition a team *gains* possession of the ball, its first challenge is to look for an immediate scoring opportunity and take it. However, this is not the most common situation in a transition, and so the key for the offense is to create space by spreading out so that the player in possession has multiple options.

If on the other hand the result of the turnover is a *loss* of possession, the first task for the defensive team is to get as many players as it can between the now attacking team and the scoring target. This way at least the goal will not be open and available for an easy shot. The other challenge is to try to deny space—to occupy the important lanes so that the attacking players do not become open targets within the offensive scheme.

Sample Invasion Games

The games outlined in this section are arranged in an order in which their tactical complexity increases. The goal is to highlight different ways of playing and to play games that underscore a particular strategy or innovative design feature.

Planet Escape

The first two games in this section do not involve manipulating an object; instead, they introduce the concepts of penetrating into space and denying possession, which are so important to success in invasion games. Planet escape is based on the game Planet Invasion created by Reginald S. Kimball (http://pecentral.com/lessonideas/ViewLesson.asp?ID=691).

PLAYERS

6 or 7 players per side

EQUIPMENT

12 small cones or blocks, 2 hoops

ORGANIZATION

Set up the playing area by dividing the gym into two sides with 6 small cones at each end of the playing field. Set up two hoops near the centerline (but near the side), one on each side of the playing area.

Each team starts on its own half of the court.

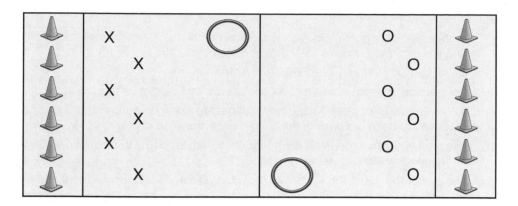

Setup for planet escape.

RULES

▶ The objective of the game is to get as many of the opposing team's cones as possible without getting touched.

▶ When you obtain a cone, you get a free trip back to your own side.

▶ If you get touched you have to go to "jail" (where the hoops are set up).

▶ To get out, one of your teammates must come and tag you without getting touched himself.

▶ If your teammate does get touched, he has to go into the hoop as well, but if he does not, then both people get a free trip back to their own side.

▶ At the end of a designated time limit, the team with the most cones wins.

VARIATIONS

▶ Allow each team to place the cones along the baseline in positions they consider most tactically advantageous.

▶ Manipulate the number of designated taggers.

▶ Add more hoops.

Used by permission of PE Central (www.pecentral.org), the premier web site for physical education teachers.

Flip the Frisbees

Like planet escape, this game emphasizes penetrating into space and denying possession.

PLAYERS

6 players per side

EQUIPMENT

20 Frisbees, 10 hoops

ORGANIZATION

Scatter 5 hoops and 10 Frisbees on each half of the court. The hoops act as safe bases. On each Frisbee, tape a number from 1 to 10 on the back, and lay it facedown.

RULES

- ▶ The objective of the game is to run into the other team's side and flip over the Frisbees to score points. (All Frisbees have different point values from 1 to 10).
- ▶ A player can flip over only one Frisbee at a time.
- ▶ If a player has one foot inside a hoop, she is safe and cannot be tagged.
- ▶ Once the Frisbee has been flipped over, the person is safe to return to her side of the court but must go to the back of the court before returning to play.
- ▶ There are two taggers on each team, and if you are tagged you must return to your side. Taggers must stay outside the hoops.
- ▶ At the end of the game the team with the most points will win, or the team that flips over all the Frisbees first wins and the game is reset and begins again (with people changing roles from defense to offense).

VARIATIONS

- ▶ Allow each team to place the hoops and Frisbees on its court in places considered most tactically advantageous.
- ▶ Repeat this, but with teams placing the hoops and Frisbees that *they* will be retrieving anywhere in their opponent's half.
- ▶ After trying these variations, students may decide to place limits on the placement rules after a game, as various options may prove unworkable (such as a team placing all the Frisbees in one corner).

Line Ball

Line ball is a simple invasion game where two teams of four each try to score by passing a ball to a teammate over an end line.

PLAYERS

4 players per side

EQUIPMENT

Soft Nerf-like ball that players can hold in one hand, 8 cones to mark the boundaries of the court

ORGANIZATION

The size of each court can vary depending upon the skill and experience of the players. You could fit three courts side by side running the length of a basketball court.

RULES

- ▶ Team 1 will start from a designated spot. On the signal, the players will attempt to move the ball down the court by throwing to teammates.
- ▶ If the ball is caught, the team will maintain possession.
- ▶ If the ball is dropped, batted down, or intercepted, the other team gains possession.
- ▶ If the player with the ball tags the defender, he must run and touch a wall to come back into the game.
- ▶ Players are not allowed to remain in their opponent's end zone for more than three seconds. If a player has been in the end zone, she may not return to the end zone until a teammate has entered it.
- ▶ The ultimate goal is to cross the designated end line. As soon as a point is scored, the ball is dropped and team 2 will have possession.

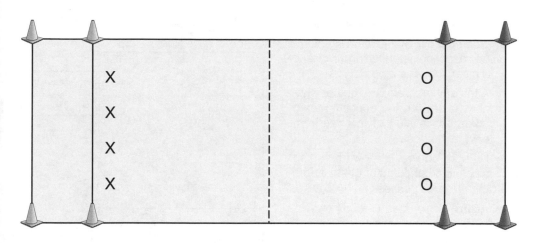

Setup for line ball.

VARIATIONS

▶ **Everyone scores.** Continue using the same basic rules for line ball, but play is for a total of five minutes. The goal of both teams is to have each of its players score at least one time. For example, if team 1 is ahead 8-4 at the end of 5 minutes but player 4 has not scored, then team 2 would be the winning team.

▶ **One-man show.** In this format, one person from each team can score points. Each team will select one member to be its scorer. The point does not count if any other member catches the ball beyond the end line. This game in particular requires teams to use ball movement to help get the scorer open and to use screens as a method of getting players open.

Zone Ball

This game shows how limiting players to specific areas on a court opens up play.

PLAYERS

5 players per side (play as many games as needed so all students in the class are participating)

EQUIPMENT

Large playground ball or basketball, 2 large buckets or open boxes

ORGANIZATION

The size of each court can vary depending upon the skill and experience of the players. You could fit three courts side by side running the length of a basketball court.

RULES

▶ The court is divided into two sections. Each team must have two defenders and two attackers. These players cannot cross the halfway line. Each team also has one rover, who can go anywhere on the court.

▶ Progression of the ball is only by passing. No dribbling or running with the ball.

▶ An attacker in possession has two options: (1) pass or (2) shoot at the goal. If the attacker wishes to shoot at the goal, he must call out, "Shooting!" and cannot make a pass to a teammate.

▶ The rover can also be a shooter.

▶ Once the attacker calls, "Shooting!" he cannot be defended and can take a clear shot at the goal.

▶ After a shot attempt (whether successful or not), the opposing team takes possession of the ball from next to the goal.

▶ No body contact is allowed, and no stealing or stripping of the ball from the player in possession is allowed.

▶ After a designated time, all players must swap one position.

VARIATIONS

▶ Vary the size of the balls—this will change the way the ball is thrown.

▶ If you are playing inside, you may use a target on the wall instead of a goal.

▶ For extra challenge, the ball may have to remain *in* the bucket to be a goal.

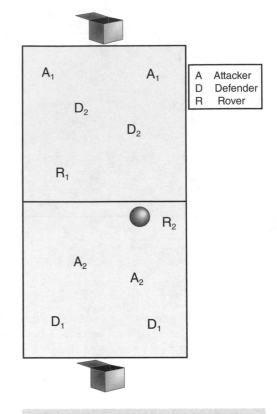

A	Attacker
D	Defender
R	Rover

Setup for zone ball.

Corridor Ball

This game allows for varying levels of defensive pressure to be incorporated for difficult skills.

PLAYERS

5 players per side (play as many games as needed so all students in the class are participating)

EQUIPMENT

Cones or tape to designate scoring zone, whatever equipment you are to play with (e.g., soccer ball, hockey stick and ball, short-handled lacrosse stick)

ORGANIZATION

The size of each court can vary depending upon the skill and experience of the players. You could fit three courts side by side running the length of a basketball court.

RULES

▶ The court is divided into three sections. The outer "corridors" are one-way traffic for the designated team. Only one offensive player and no defensive players can be in a corridor at any time.

▶ Progression of the ball in the main court is by passing only. However, in a corridor, the player may use whatever skills are relevant to the game (e.g., dribbling the soccer ball or hockey puck, running with the lacrosse ball).

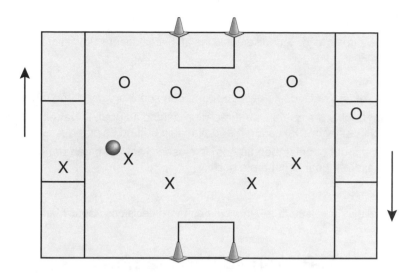

► Scoring is achieved by passing the ball to a teammate in the scoring box. Anyone can pass to this player. Only one attacking player and no defenders can be in the goal.

► The player in the corridor can progress with the ball across *one* line. That is, that player cannot move down the entire length of the court.

► The corridor player must pass the ball to a teammate within a designated period of time (players decide)—this is to prevent stalling.

► After a pass from the corridor, that player must leave and move to the main court. No player can be in the corridor on two consecutive possessions.

► No body contact is allowed, and no stealing or stripping of the ball from the player in possession is allowed.

► After a designated time, all players must swap one position.

VARIATIONS

► Depending on the game being simulated, change the scoring requirements.

► Allow teams to use either corridor to progress the ball.

Pin Soccer

This game helps players to analyze attacking opportunities by having multiple and simultaneous attack options. Having four teams playing at the one time encourages a quick flow from attack to defense and also encourages the concept of overloading defensive pressure, as would be the case if two teams simultaneously attack one goal.

PLAYERS

4 players per side, with 4 teams playing concurrently

EQUIPMENT

Cones for boundaries, 12 bowling pins

ORGANIZATION

Place four different goals at the four different sides of a large square playing area. Behind each goal place three pins.

RULES

▶ Each team of four defends its own goal and can score on any of the other three.

▶ Each team begins the game with three pins behind its goal. If team 1 scores a goal on team 2, then team 1 takes a pin and places it behind its goal.

▶ If a team runs out of pins, then its goal is closed. That team can bring its goalie out and try to score a goal to get a pin back.

VARIATION

Play with two balls at the same time—this creates more decisions about whether to attack or defend.

Poor Invasion Games

Although invasion games would appear to be designed to keep all players very active, there is still the potential for some participants to be standing and waiting. Games in which this occurs are usually those where either the field is too large or there are too many players. One of the major challenges when designing invasion games is to get the playing number just right. Quite simply, experimentation with the size of the field is best when the player number is less flexible, while exploring different playing numbers is best when the boundaries are less adaptable.

Some invasion games have rules that allow a single player or two to dominate all phases of play. Although the use of zones and possession rules can offer some assistance, it is not always a problem with the rules, just that some players have really mastered the skills and tactics of the game. An alternative to making a whole-game rule change for when one team achieves a predetermined advantage over its opponents (e.g., a difference of 10 points or 5 goals) is to incorporate a challenge box. In these situations, the high-scoring team must take a challenge card from a challenge box and comply with its rule. An example in a basketball-type game might be "You must receive and pass within two seconds." The objective of the challenge is to stretch the tactics of the winning team while shifting some advantage toward the team that is trailing on the scoreboard. If the gap in the score between the two teams doubles, then a new challenge card must be taken. If the score evens out, the challenged team may revert to normal play. A fun part of designing invasion games is to consider potential challenges without losing the integrity of the game itself.

Safety in Invasion Games

By their very nature, invasion games involve a lot of potential for collisions because there are situations where players are quickly changing directions as well as dodging and faking, stopping and starting. It is important when designing invasion games that first of all, sufficient space is provided in the dimensions of the field so that players can spread out and move comfortably about the area.

Particular attention must be taken of the relationship between an end wall and the baseline of a game. If end walls are close to the baseline, protective gym mats or padding will need to be used. In cases where a stage is close to the baseline, padding will need to be put over the edge of the stage that extends to the floor.

The other area of potential collision is between a player and an implement. In games such as hockey and lacrosse where the sticks are long, games designers need to consider rules that limit the amount of backswing that a player can use. Floor hockey games often have the stipulation that the stick must remain in contact with ground (or at least below the knees), and in some cases, failure to adhere to this rule means the stick is replaced by something far less productive such as a noodle.

Rules need also be considered about how players are able to intercept or take the ball from an opponent. In most schools, it is unlikely that tackling would be allowed, and it makes sense from an inclusive perspective (i.e., what makes a good game) that tackling is not selected. However, there are other situations that can be dangerous when two players are disputing possession, and these must be modified, eliminated, or addressed in the rules of the game. For example, in lacrosse, modify the rules to exclude stick-on-stick, stick-on-body, or body-on-body contact and to prevent accidental contact within 3 feet (1 m) of the gym wall or an outside obstacle such as a fence. Likewise, if using scooter boards, do not permit scooter-to-scooter intentional contact.

In some school jurisdictions there are requirements for certain safety equipment such as eye and mouth protection. When creating games that require this equipment, games designers and their instructors must ensure the school has the appropriate inventory, or they will need to substitute equipment that does not involve the risk.

Questions to Consider When Designing Invasion Games

Because of their great diversity, it is possible to begin the design of an invasion game from a number of different angles. For some, it may be the method of scoring that finds particular attraction, while for others a particular piece of equipment used in play might be the starting point. Still again, depending upon the circumstances, invasion games designers might have to work in a particular setting (e.g., in a pool, in a gymnasium, or outdoors on ice).

No matter what the starting point, the design of invasion games will involve reflection about the three key components of all games (possession, progression, scoring). However, what is most usual is a backward sequence where issues of scoring are first examined, followed by the rules relating to progression and then possession. It is this sequence we will follow here. For ease of reading, we will use the term *ball* for the object used in scoring, acknowledging that many games use other pieces of equipment, such as pucks.

• **How do you score?** Most invasion games follow one of four scoring methods. The two most common are either to get the ball through a goal (one that is either on the ground or in the air) or to move the ball over an end line. Less frequently adopted, but equally fun, is to score by getting the ball to a team-mate in a designated place (not being an end zone) or simply to gain possession a designated number of times. It should be noted here that when planning invasion games, it is not necessary to select only one of these options. Many well-designed games have multiple scoring options that include combinations of goals and end zones.

● **How is the goal to be designed?** If an invasion game is to use a goal, four questions must be addressed. These are similar to those contemplated when designing target games, since these goals are acting as scoring targets. The four questions follow:

1. Where are we going to place the goals on the court or field? Although most invasion games have their goals on the end line, allowing play behind the goals such as is the case in ice hockey can really open up play and enhance the challenge.

2. What is their size?

3. At what height and angle will they be placed (on the ground or in the air; horizontal or vertical)?

4. How many goals will be included in the game?

The use of multiple goals certainly speeds up play and often spreads out the defense. However, if multiple goals are introduced, games designers need to structure their scoring system so that each goal is worth attacking. In some games, players ignore a goal or scoring option because it adds little value. Goals that are more challenging to score should be worth more points, but not at the expense of others, which may become redundant. Later, rules can be developed about how these goals may be attacked or defended, together with player limitations in terms of who can attack and defend.

● **How can you progress toward the goal(s)?** All invasion games will involve teams moving the ball toward the target goal. The most common methods for an individual to move toward the goal are dribbling (e.g., basketball, soccer, and hockey) and running with the ball (e.g., various football codes or lacrosse). Nonetheless, there are many other options. These may include throwing, pushing, striking, kicking, riding, or swimming. With each of these, decisions need to be made about possession limits (e.g., only three steps or two dribbles) and about the legality of passes. For example, in some games, passing can only be made backward, while in others such as ultimate Frisbee, a pass must be made without the ball touching the ground.

Allowing players to run with the ball opens up a whole new element of invasion games. It allows for quicker progression (and hence more scoring), and it places more stress on the defenders. It also allows players who are closely guarded to simply run away, thereby preventing highly skilled players from suffocating the play options of those less experienced. Although most traditional games that allow a player to run also allow defenders to tackle, there are suitable alternatives. The most common is that if players in possession are tagged they lose possession, which forces acute awareness of space. Another option is a compulsory "stop and pass" in which the player must stop progression and pass immediately to a teammate.

If game designers do not wish to allow full running, it is worthwhile for them to consider allowing one or two steps while in possession. This has a significant positive effect in games such as Frisbee where players can become more concerned with not taking steps than moving the disc quickly to a teammate.

• **How do you get possession?** In typical invasion games, while one team is progressing, its opponent will be trying to get possession. In the active situation (i.e., while the team has the ball), the other team can gain possession directly by intercepting and dispossessing. Intercepting can include cutting off a pass from one player to another, or it might be a case where the player in possession loses control of the ball. Dispossessing can be achieved through physically stripping the player of the ball (tackling) or performing some other action (e.g., tagging or stealing a tag belt) that will result in the turnover. Decisions about interceptions and tackling need to be addressed when designing invasion games.

Possession can also change in other situations. The most common situation is when one team scores, its opponent gains possession. However, teams may get possession if their opponents send the ball out of play, if they have completed their allotted number of possessions (think of American football and rugby league), or if they violate one of the game's rules. In all cases, however, a decision will need to be made as to where the team will get possession of the ball.

• **How physical should play be?** Often it is difficult for games designers to make a decision on how *physical* the game should be played. In physical education, it is certainly prudent to not allow students to design games that are excessively rough. This is sensible from a safety perspective, and in addition, games that favor those who are fortunate enough to be bigger and stronger are counterproductive when we are trying to take advantage of all students' skills and abilities.

Tag belts offer a means of dispossession.

Stage 3 defense: Feet can move, but no arms.

The four levels of defense continuum can help games makers decide on an appropriate level of stress to be placed on those in possession. In order, these are as follows:

- Stage 1: feet still, arms still
- Stage 2: feet still, arms move
- Stage 3: feet move, arms still behind back
- Stage 4: full guarding

If full guarding is to be used, a very useful rule can be incorporated to open up play. Simply, if the player in possession tags a defender, that defender must then run to the side of the court or field before reengaging in the play. This simple rule avoids situations where players in possession are overaggressively guarded or double-teamed. Used well, the rule can also be put to good use by attackers when they are close to scoring.

• **How to resume after a score?** As mentioned, one way to gain possession is to be given the ball after a score. However, a possession change need not be the only outcome. In games such as netball, possession alternates from the center circle following a goal, irrespective of who scored. In Australian football, after a 6-point score, the umpire bounces the ball in the center circle, while in ice hockey the players face off.

Games designers should also consider whether there is any need for a restart after a score. In some games, especially where teams score by hitting a target, it might be just as beneficial to continue play, with possession going to the team that retrieves the ball first after the shot on goal. If the goal is missed, then there is no consequence. Play just simulates a rebound. If the goal is hit, the attacking team is responsible for resetting it correctly. It is in their interest to do so quickly as they cannot score again until the goal is restored.

• **How to begin the game or a period of play?** Given that invasion games involve possession, someone has to have the first turn with the ball. A jump ball or face-off can be used, or the choice of possession may be determined after a coin toss. In some games, teams may specifically want to defend first, and so games designers will need to consider the options a team has if it wins the toss.

• **What is the playing area and its boundaries?** With few exceptions (e.g., Australian rules football), nearly all invasion games are played on rectangular courts or fields. However, this is not something that is set in stone, and creative games designers may find another shape that is particularly attractive for their game. Of course, the first question that needs to be asked is whether boundaries are necessary at all.

Other primary decisions will include whether the game is more suited to indoor or outdoor play. If indoor, will there be sidelines on the court, or will players be able to use the wall? If the wall comes into play, in what capacity can it be utilized? Where boundaries are implemented, decisions need to be made about how the ball is to be put in play once it has gone out.

The next phase is to decide how the court or field will be marked with regard to zones. The zones can relate to scoring or to limitations of players' movements. For example, in both field hockey and netball, the ball must be in a certain zone before a score attempt can be made. In basketball, shots made within the 3-point line are worth 2, and those from outside are worth 3.

With regard to players' movements, games such as team handball have areas in which only one defensive player and no attacking players are allowed. The game of netball is divided into thirds, and while different players can be in different areas, no player has access to the entire court.

● **What balls and implements will be used?** The beauty of invasion games is that you are almost unlimited in the choice of playing equipment. Any object that can be passed between players will suffice. From the familiar Frisbee to the more distinctive buzkashi, many games makers have gone out of their way to find a creative new challenge.

Buzkashi, which literally translated means "goat grabbing," is the national sport of Afghanistan. In buzkashi, the headless carcass of a goat is placed in the center of a circle and surrounded by players on horseback of two opposing teams. The objective of the game is to get control of the carcass and bring it to the scoring area. In one version of the game, the player must carry the carcass around a marker and then return it to the team's designated scoring circle. Points

A Word on the Center Line and Direction of Play

All traditional invasion games involve teams traveling in one direction, usually with a change at the end of a period of play. However, there is nothing to say that games must follow this convention. Indeed, many exciting and strategically challenging games have been developed in which teams can score at either end. The rule of play best included in such a case is listed as follows: Once a team gains possession, it must cross the halfway line before it can score. After crossing the halfway line, the team is free to score at either end. That is, if team A was attacking the right end zone but loses possession, team B can now pass to cross the halfway line and continue to the left, or reverse play and make a scoring attempt at the end in which team A was previously attacking.

This rule serves to significantly spread out defenses and open up scoring. However, it also has the advantage in that players can alternate very quickly from being in an attacking position to a defensive one. The game of ultimate Frisbee golf (see chapter 10) is a good example of either-end scoring.

Buzkashi is an example of the creative use of resources in invasion games.

are awarded for successfully completing the task of getting control of the carcass and getting it to the proper scoring area.

The nature of this game also reinforces the idea that play need not be unidirectional.

Although creativity might drive the original intent of games designers, pragmatic decisions such as the availability of resources (e.g., slaughtered goats) will nonetheless come into play. With regard to balls, the choices are still numerous. The first question will be "What is the shape of the ball?" Round balls are easy to pass, dribble, and shoot, while oval balls are easier to catch, travel farther when kicked, and add an element of uncertainty when they hit the ground. Sports goods companies are now producing other shapes of balls, with pyramid balls and others with dimples now readily available.

The second question will be "How large and compact will the ball be?" The size and density of a ball will also affect its suitability for play. Smaller balls are easier to throw but perhaps harder to catch, while larger balls may be easier to catch and dribble but are more easily stolen by a defender. Firmer balls are easier to throw, while softer balls are more easily caught. Firmer balls are usually more accurate, but softer balls are more appropriate in cases where there is a goalkeeper or if the ball is thrown at players. No matter the ball chosen for play, in all cases there are trade-offs and compromises.

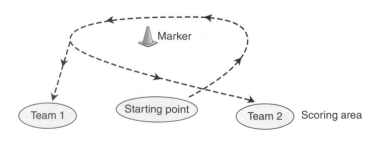

Setup for buzkashi.

As mentioned already, not all invasion games use a ball, and many use pieces of equipment in addition to the object that is advanced. Consider hockey in all its forms or lacrosse. In these games a stick is used to hit, carry, or dribble the puck or ball. One game designed by some students at a school in England used milk jugs in which a ball was carried and scooped rather than thrown. Pool noodles were also used as accessories, either to dribble the ball, retrieve it into the milk jug, or tag an opponent. Games designers need to consider whether theirs will be a ball-only game or one that uses additional implements.

- **What to do about faults and penalties?** Given they can be complex games, there will be many situations in invasion games where players violate one of the rules. As a starting point in games making, it is helpful for teams to delineate their rules in terms of possession, progression, and scoring. From this point they can ask three questions: (1) What is a foul? (2) What happens if the foul is accidental? (3) What happens if the foul is deliberate?

A Template for Designing Invasion Games

Table 7.1 provides a template of decisions that can be given to games makers when they are about to design an invasion game. Table 7.2 on page 97 presents the game of cone ball using the key design questions.

TABLE 7.1—Template for Designing Invasion Games	
Design question	**Options**
How do you score?	Goal (air or ground)
	Ball to person in a certain place
	Gain possession
	Move ball over a line
How can you progress up the court or field?	Pass
	Throw
	Run
	Push
	Strike
	Dribble
	Kick
	Ride
	Swim
What object are you going to use to score?	Ball (various sizes, shapes, and densities)
	Puck
	Flag, sock, beanbag
	Person only
	Animal (simulated!)

From P. Hastie, 2010, *Student-Designed Games: Strategies for Promoting Creativity, Cooperation, and Skill Development* (Champaign, IL: Human Kinetics).

(continued)

TABLE 7.1 *(continued)*

Design question	Options
What implement will be used to move the object?	Scoop to carry the ball Stick to hit the ball
How do you get possession?	After a score Interception Tackle or tag Fumble or strip Rebound Violation Out of play Opposition has no more turns
How do you start the game or begin a new period?	Tip-off Face-off Designated receiver Coin toss for possession Shoot-off
What are the boundaries?	None Sidelines only Walled in Shape (various)
What are the goals?	Size Shape Location Angle Number
How do you resume play following a score?	Simply continue (play does not stop) Possession to opponent Jump ball Face-off Throw-in by referee Alternate possession
What are the consequences of rule violations?	Faults or penalties Break progression rule Break possession rule Break scoring rule

From P. Hastie, 2010, *Student-Designed Games: Strategies for Promoting Creativity, Cooperation, and Skill Development* (Champaign, IL: Human Kinetics).

TABLE 7.2—Cone Ball

Design question	Solutions
How do you score?	A point is scored each time the target ball falls off its supporting cone. The attacking team can hit the ball directly or simply hit the cone and dislodge the ball. If a defending player accidentally knocks the ball from the cone, this is also a score for the attacking team.
How can you progress up the court or field?	Players may run in any direction and for any distance while in possession of the ball. They may also throw it to a teammate. The pass does not have to be so that the ball does not touch the ground. That is, it is possible to roll the ball or drop it and then kick it to a teammate. If a player in possession is tagged (irrespective of whether he is running or not), possession changes to the tagger, who then can make one throw (but not run) without being tagged. If the tagger begins to run, he may then be tagged.
What objects are you going to use to score?	Given the goalkeeper will be the recipient of many direct hits, the playing ball is a loosely inflated "nubby" ball (a soft-touch inflatable ball about 10 in. [25 cm] in diameter with a foamlike cover featuring tactile bumps).
What implement will be used to move the object?	No implements are used. Players can use any part of their body to move the ball.
How do you get possession?	Possession can be achieved four ways: (1) by tagging a player in possession, (2) by retrieving the ball after a shot on goal, (3) by intercepting a pass, or (4) by recovering a loose ball.
How do you start the game or begin a new period?	Play starts in possession of the goalkeeper of the team who wins the toss.
What are the boundaries?	The goal zone is a square around the free-throw line of a basketball court, but there are no other specific boundaries. Play is limited only by whatever obstructions there are in the vicinity of the playing space (e.g., side and end walls). Shots on goal must be from outside the goal zone, and only one defender is allowed inside this area.
What are the goals?	The goal consists of a ball sitting atop a small cone. The ball should be small enough so that it falls off when either it or the cone is hit. The traffic cone should have a hollow top to allow a small crevice for the ball to sit in.
How do you resume play following a score?	Play does not stop after a successful shot at the target. The loose ball is available for either team to collect. The successful team, however, must replace the ball on top of the cone and reset the cone if it is either knocked over or out of place.
What are the consequences of rule violations?	The only faults are continuing to run after being tagged or excessively rough tagging. For both of these, the infringed team has a free shot at the cone from the point of the foul.

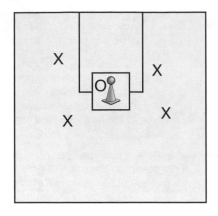

Setup for cone ball.

Nubby balls.

Conclusion

Invasion games are probably the most diverse of all the game forms. Although all contain the elements of possession, progression, and scoring, there are almost unlimited ways in which these can be combined to create a new game. This may explain the preponderance of invasion games that exist in the formal sports culture. Nonetheless, there is still plenty of scope for new invasion games. All that is needed is an uninhibited imagination.

References

Maxwell, T. (2006). A progressive decision options approach to coaching invasion games: Basketball as an example. *Journal of Physical Education New Zealand, 39* (1), 58-71.

Rovegno, I., Nevett, M., Brock, S., & Babiarz, M. (2001). Teaching and learning basic invasion-game tactics in 4th grade: A descriptive study from situated and constraints theoretical perspectives. *Journal of Teaching in Physical Education, 20,* 370-388.

CHAPTER 8

Striking and Fielding Games

Striking and fielding games are those in which two teams take alternate turns at attempting to accumulate runs by striking an object. A run is usually defined as a successful progression from one point to another following a designated pathway. In games such as softball, baseball, and rounders, which have curved pathways, players can stop at various points on the way to scoring. In other games such as cricket, which uses a straight pathway, there is no such opportunity. However, in the case of cricket, a batter can make more than one run at a time. The judgment in all these cases, however, involves a decision about the safety of making it to the next point.

Striking and fielding games of all types have a number of similarities. First, the teams alternate after a certain number of outs. In softball and baseball, the number is 3, while in cricket it is 10 (unless the batting team decides it wants to finish for time reasons). Still, in other games such as kastie it is a one-out-all-out situation. The second similarity is that all striking and fielding games involve striking skills, and the implement is nearly always called a bat. Of course, the shape, weight, and size of these bats vary (and in some games the player's hand can be used), but the fundamental goal of the player who is striking is to hit the ball away from the fielding team. The third similarity is that all these games involve throwing and catching skills, and failure to catch or throw accurately can have adverse consequences. In particular, in nearly all striking and fielding games, catching a hit ball before it lands on the ground is an out. The fourth similarity between striking and fielding games is that they are usually played outdoors on large playing areas (most often grass).

Key Principles of Striking and Fielding Games

The unique feature of striking and fielding games compared with all others is the concept of *innings*. In these games, teams take turns doing one of two roles. In invasion games, net or wall games, and tag games, the contestants are engaged simultaneously either as an attacker or a defender. In basketball, both teams are

Photo courtesy of Will Scott.

Almost anything can be used as a bat, as seen here in a game of lapta, which is popular in Russia.

trying to get the ball and score, while in tennis, both players are trying to hit the ball over the net so the opponent cannot return it. Likewise in fencing, both players are trying to tag the other before being tagged themselves.

In striking and fielding games, however, the tasks are separate and essentially opposite. Nonetheless, in both cases the primary challenge is to make life difficult for the other team. For the batting team, the major challenge is to exploit gaps in the field in order to score. For the fielding team, the goal is to close gaps in order to reduce scoring opportunities.

Required Experiences for Success in Striking and Fielding Games

All striking and fielding games involve the skills of throwing and catching, pitching (or bowling), hitting, moving to intercept the ball, and running. Hence, games players will need experiences in all of these components in order to both master the skills and appreciate the relevance of those skills to the specific game being played.

THROWING

Students will need skills in throwing for accuracy and also throwing over long distances. Throwing for accuracy should be practiced using both overhand and underhand techniques, and particularly with regard to underhand throws, with right and left hands. Throwing for accuracy should include throwing to partners and also throwing at targets. Those targets should be of different sizes, distances, and heights. The importance of using appropriate force should also be encouraged, especially in games where the fielding team does not wear gloves. When practicing throwing to targets (either object or person), the skills of backing up should also be developed.

All throwing tasks should be practiced under various time stresses. Initially, throwing can be practiced without the need to beat the runner, but later, as ball-handling skills improve, it is valuable to introduce tasks where the fielding player needs to get rid of the ball quickly. A second time stress can be introduced that involves recognition of *where* to throw. That is, minigames can be played where fielders have to make decisions about which base or point to throw to. These decisions can be based upon the situation of the game (e.g., how many batters are out) or the location of the runners (e.g., which is farthest from being safe, or which is more likely to score).

CATCHING

In nearly all striking and fielding games, to catch a hit ball is to make an out. Consequently, catching is a fundamental skill. It is important that players get catching experiences in a full range of opportunities, as in striking and fielding games there are different roles for the fielding team: catcher or wicket keeper, short fielders, base fielders, and deep fielders.

Students should be given experiences in tracking the flight of a ball—first in catching balls that are coming toward them and they have to move forward, and then in catching balls that are going over their heads. Here they need to decide whether to simply back up to catch or whether to turn and run.

Students can also benefit from catching activities where the ball is arriving to them at various heights. The positioning of the hands relative to the flight of the ball (i.e., thumbs up for a high ball and thumbs down for a low ball) should also be practiced.

PITCHING OR BOWLING

In all striking and fielding games, the ball must be delivered to the batter by an overhand or underhand throw, or by using a bowling action. In most adult forms of these games, the pitcher or bowler can record an out by hitting a specific target. If this option is selected in a student-designed game, then time needs to be allocated to practice the selected skill.

A good pitcher or bowler should use a variety of deliveries in order to exploit the weaknesses of each batter. Students should therefore be given experiences in pitching and bowling to develop accuracy and, later, to change the pace of the delivery and impart different spins to the ball.

HITTING

Like catching and throwing, all striking and fielding games involve putting the ball in play. While using mostly, but not exclusively, a bat,

Batting practice is essential for good game play.

Photo courtesy of Mat Skene.

students will need to practice at hitting for accuracy so they can then place the ball to various parts of the field. And in some games where running is not required on contact, specific practice of defensive shots appropriate to that game would be helpful.

For students to be true masters of batting, they should be able to select the best shot for the type of delivery received. Practice can be taken where batters adjust their strokes to the pace and bounce and maybe the spin of the pitch. Practice should also include hitting balls along the ground and in the air.

INTERCEPTING AND COLLECTING

Students need practice at intercepting and collecting (the two components most commonly called fielding). *Intercepting* is defined as getting in the appropriate position to cut off the ball. The approach to the ball might be front on (if the ball is hit directly toward the fielder) but more likely will be from the side (as batters usually try to hit toward gaps). Students can design and practice small challenge games where they play one on one, trying to score by getting the ball past each other with an underhand toss or roll.

Once the player is in position to intercept the ball, the actual collecting or gathering of the ball follows. The decision to pick up the ball with either one or both hands will also be determined by many factors, including the bounce and speed of the ball as well as the importance of being able to get rid of the ball quickly.

RUNNING

To be a totally accomplished striking and fielding games player, students will need experiences in running. In some games the bat is carried while running (e.g., cricket, stoolball), while in others it is dropped before running (e.g., baseball, softball). Nonetheless, players need to know the appropriate methods of running for their particular game. In particular, practice should be included that focuses on how to change direction while either running the bases or running from point to point in a straight line. Beginning cricket players should always be given instruction about how to correctly ground the bat and turn for a second run.

Students should also have experience in games that include decisions about whether or not they should run. These tasks ought to help students understand how the placement of the fielders will affect their potential to run to safety. Instructors should also encourage students to recognize how the handedness of the fielder (i.e., does this fielder throw with his right or left hand?) will affect how quickly he can release the ball. From a more aggressive perspective, batters should learn and experience situations where they can put fielders under pressure with their running between bases. Finally, students should have some experiences developing response plans to misfielded or dropped catches.

In some games where two batters must work together to score (such as in cricket), they will need to practice calling "yes" for a run, "no" to refuse a run, and "wait" to see what happens before a yes or no call. "Sorry" can be reserved for mistakes, but discourage calls such as "go" as it sounds too much like no. Loud, confident calls are important, so get the players to shout.

Key Strategies for Success in Striking and Fielding Games

From a tactical perspective, striking and fielding games can be divided into defensive (fielding) and offensive (striking or batting) strategies, and these can be examined from a team or an individual angle. We will begin with the defensive strategies first, as this is where play begins, with the delivery of the ball. However, you can be aggressive in offense by seeking runs or defensive by taking only the surest of options. Likewise, when fielding you can close the field or open the field as appropriate.

FIELDING STRATEGIES

The primary strategic goal for the fielding team is to limit the ability of the batting team to score. This is most likely achieved if the fielding team can make the batting team hit the ball to where the fielding team has placed its players. This can be accomplished in three ways. First, from an anticipatory perspective, the fielders can look for clues in the striker's setup as to where the hit will go.

Second, the fielding team can deliver the ball to the batter so the only option is to hit it to spaces covered by fielders. This can be done by either exploiting a certain space in the batting zone (e.g., either one side or the other of the batter, or close to or far from the batter) or by pitching or bowling to a batter's weakness. Some batters have trouble hitting the ball when it is high in the striking zone; others struggle when the ball is delivered low. Some batters are more affected by the outright pace of the ball, while others can hit a fast-pitched ball but struggle with a change of pace or spin. All of these factors will limit where the batter can hit the ball and will dictate the subsequent location of the fielders.

Third, and on a more defensive note, a fielding team can recognize that a batter has a particular strength and will place its fielders in the areas most favored by the batter. Likewise, fielding teams will make adjustments based upon whether the batters are left or right handed.

In some batting games, it is possible to select which batter you want to pitch or bowl to. In games with two batters such as cricket, a team may attempt to keep one of the two players facing the bowling, while the other remains at the nonscoring end. Although at times this may mean giving up a run to the better batter, the trade-off lies in an enhanced ability to get the weaker batter out or to restrict scoring. In games such as baseball and softball, a team may chose to give the batter a base without having to hit. In these cases the decision is based upon a belief that the team can get the next batter out, or that the batter given a free pass was capable of scoring a lot of runs. In student-designed games, players may want to be aware of this free-base situation and incorporate rules so that the better players do not find themselves never getting to bat.

BATTING STRATEGIES

The key strategies for the batting team are to hit where the fielding team has not covered—the open spaces. These open spaces do not necessarily have to be to the far corners of the field. In fact, a productive shot might be a gentle hit such as

The bunt is one way to hit to open spaces.

a bunt. Many skilled batters have mastered the art of dropping the ball at their feet and scampering quickly to a base.

In order to hit to an open space, a batter will first have to decide whether to hit the pitch or leave it. As we have noted, in some games, you don't have to run on contact, and so this decision to hit or leave will vary between games such as cricket and softball. Players can be more defensive in games where there is not a hit and run rule.

If, however, the decision is to hit the ball, the batter needs to decide how to hit it. Players need to appreciate that if they hit the ball in the air they run the risk of being caught out, but these lofted hits are often higher scoring if successful.

Sample Striking and Fielding Games

Striking and fielding games typically are played on either fan-shaped fields where the striking team always hits forward or on oval-shaped fields where the batters are in the center of the field and can hit in any direction. The traditional games in these categories often involve large numbers, resulting in the potential for players to go long periods between turns whether they are fielding or batting. The games that follow are designed to maximize participation without compromising the tactical dimensions of the games. In fact, these games are more likely to highlight specific tactical challenges than their parent version.

FIELDING

The first two games in this section place a focus on the fielding team. Given that the ball will almost always be put in play, it is up to the fielders to make adjustments depending upon where the runners will be and who is up to bat.

Five-a-Side Softball

PLAYERS

5 players per side

EQUIPMENT

3 hoops for bases, a bat, and a RagBall-type softball

ORGANIZATION

Set up the three bases (home, first, and second) in a triangle.

RULES

▶ The striking team pitches to its own players (there is no restriction on where this pitch is made from).

▶ The ball must be hit into fair territory within two swings or the batter is out (includes air swings).

▶ The ball must hit the ground *before* passing the imaginary (or chalked) line linking first and second base.

▶ Once the ball is in play, all other softball rules apply (i.e., with regard to base running, force and tag plays, and fly ball rules).

▶ After three outs, the teams change roles.

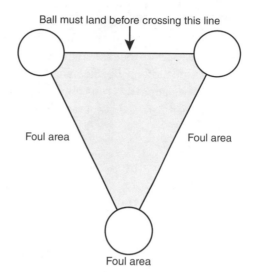

Setup for five-a-side softball.

VARIATIONS

▶ In the fourth inning, teams can select one player's turn in which she is exempt from the requirement to hit a ground ball.

▶ In the fifth inning, teams can select one player, and *each* time that player bats he is exempt.

▶ After the fifth inning, all players are exempt from the hitting restriction.

Over-the-Line Wiffle Ball

PLAYERS

2 players per side

EQUIPMENT

Wiffle ball bat and ball, cones for zone markers

ORGANIZATION

Mark an inverted triangle-shaped field for each game with cones. The apex of the triangle is home plate, and the sides represent foul lines. Divide the triangle in half with a line of chalk or more cones (this is the midline).

RULES

▶ Both defensive players stand in the outfield behind the midline.

▶ The batter receives the pitch from her teammate.

▶ Each player gets two pitches, and the offensive players take turns striking until their team gets three outs.

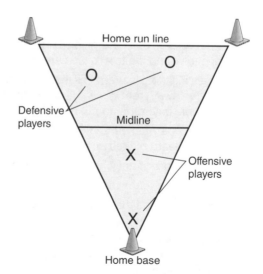

Setup for over-the-line Wiffle ball.

▶ The defensive players must prevent the ball from going over the midline. If the ball is caught in the air, it is an out.

▶ Scoring is as follows:
  – If the ball passes both lines, it is a home run.
  – The players must keep track of where their own base runners are.
  – There are only doubles and home runs.
  – Maximum of five runs per inning, then teams switch.
  – If the ball travels over the midline but is stopped before the home run line, it's a double.

HITTING

In these games, the batting team will make decisions about how to hit the ball (with regard to force and location) and also where to hit the ball (with regard to the placement of the fielders). In all three games, a key decision will be whether to hit softly or firmly.

Hoop Softball

PLAYERS

4 or 5 players per side

EQUIPMENT

Softball bat, tennis ball, 1 hoop, striking tee, 3 cones as bases

ORGANIZATION

The distance between bases can be modified according to the skill and experience of the players. Set up the fields so that all batters are hitting outward from the center.

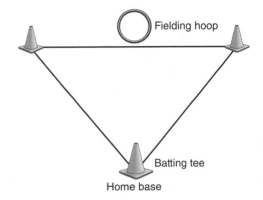

Setup for hoop softball.

RULES

▶ Each player on the striking team gets one turn, and the total bases are tallied.

▶ The striking team tries to hit the ball from the tee away from the fielders and then run around the three cone bases as fast as possible before being put out.

▶ Each cone passed scores 1 point. The player keeps running the triangle until the fielding team makes an out.

▶ Players can hit anywhere in front of the tee as a fair ball.

▶ The fielding team can be anywhere on the field.

▶ One player has the hoop, which is used to get the striking team out.

▶ To score an out, the fielders must collect the ball and then toss it from one team member to another through the hoop. So this involves three fielders: a thrower, a hoop holder, and a catcher. The player who catches the ball yells out, "Catch!" and the batter then counts the bases made.

▶ If the ball is dropped, it must be thrown back through the hoop again until it is caught.

▶ The person with the hoop is allowed to run with it.

▶ Catching a fly ball does not constitute an out. The ball must be thrown through the hoop for an out.

VARIATION

▶ Allow the striking and fielding teams to place the hoop anywhere before each batter.

▶ Alternate this option per innings (i.e., let fielding teams decide in one inning, and then let striking teams decide where to lay the hoop in the next inning).

▶ Do not allow fielders to run with the ball.

Stoolball

PLAYERS

The full-sided game has 11 on each team, but for modified purposes, teams of 5 or 6 work well.

EQUIPMENT

▶ The target is a square piece of wood at head or shoulder height fastened to a post. (Traditionally the seat of a stool hung from a post or tree was used.)

▶ A large cone to act as a base.

▶ The ball is a very soft ball, around the size of a tennis ball.

▶ The bat is a frying-pan-shaped paddle (a pickleball paddle would be excellent).

ORGANIZATION

Set up the target post and the base about 45 feet (14 m) apart, depending upon the strength of the hitters and the type of ball you use. Use field paint (or floor tape if

Playing stoolball.

Photo courtesy of Paul Williams.

playing indoors) to mark a bowling crease about 10 feet (3 m) in front of the base. This is the point from where the ball is delivered to the batter.

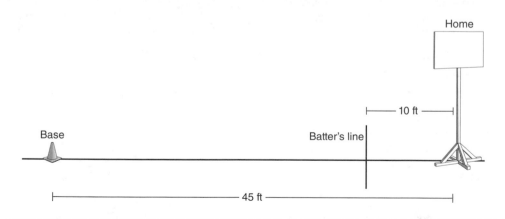

Setup for stoolball.

RULES

▶ There are no strikes or balls. The batter stays at bat until a hit is made or the pitcher hits the home target post with the ball.

▶ Any contact is a hit. There are no fouls or foul tips.

▶ On hitting the ball, the batter must run counterclockwise *around the outside* of the base. The batter may not stop on the base—once he starts running, he has to run around the base and all the way back home. The player must touch the home target when he gets there, but he doesn't have to touch the base.

▶ Batter is out when
   – the pitcher hits home with the ball while the batter is at bat;
   – any fielder catches the hit ball in the air, without a bounce; or
   – any fielder hits home with the ball while the batter is running to base and back to home.

▶ But . . .
   – Fielders must be on the base side of the line when throwing the ball at the home target. So if the batter hits the ball behind home (what in baseball would be a *foul*), the batter runs, and the fielder can go get the ball, but she can't throw it at home and put the batter out until she gets back on the other (base) side of the line.
   – Every player on the team gets one turn at bat per inning. Each team gets the same number of innings at bat, but other than that the game can go on until the teams mutually agree to quit.

VARIATION

The field dimensions aren't strict. This is just a suggested size. The game can be played in a smaller area or even indoors, though it's harder to score runs on a smaller field.

Circle Smash

PLAYERS

5 or 6, depending upon the playing space

EQUIPMENT

1 large traffic cone, short- or long-handled foam bat, 1 tennis-ball-sized no-bounce ball, 4 small cones, poly spots

ORGANIZATION

Create four concentric circles using the poly spots, and place the traffic cone in the very center circle. Use the small cones to create four equidistant bases around the second circle. The center circle should be about 4 feet (1.2 m) in radius, and the distance to the second circle is about 15 feet (4.5 m).

RULES

▶ The batter hits the ball from the large traffic cone. The hit can be in any direction, and the batter can move with the bat.

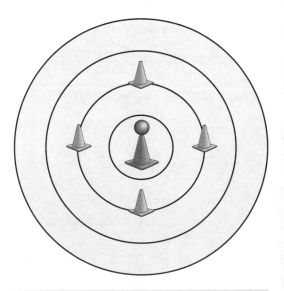

Setup for circle smash.

- ► The fielders can be in any position outside the first circle.
- ► Following the hit, the batter runs around the bases until the fielders retrieve the ball and hit the large cone.
- ► Fielders can run with the ball or pass it but cannot enter the smallest circle.
- ► The batter scores points for each base made (e.g., 1 point for first base, 2 for second, and so on) as well as a bonus score for the circle reached.
- ► Players bat in turn and keep their own individual scores.

VARIATIONS

- ► Change the dimensions of the circles.
- ► Do not allow running with the ball.

BASE RUNNING

These two games allow for significant decision making by the base runners. In both games, the runners have to be acutely aware of where the ball is located, where the fielders are positioned, and their own personal running skills.

Argoball

PLAYERS

3 to 6 players per side

EQUIPMENT

3-inch plastic ball, foam bat, 8 cones

ORGANIZATION

Create two boxes by using painter's tape or cones about 70 feet (21 m) apart. If playing on a basketball court, simply use the free-throw area. The size of each box should be about 4 feet by 4 feet (1.2 m by 1.2 m). Create a pitching line halfway between the boxes. If using a basketball court, this is the center line.

RULES

- ► The ball is pitched to a batter by a pitcher standing behind a pitching line. The batter stands anywhere within the batter's box and waits for the pitch.
- ► Only one legal pitch is made to each batter. A legal pitch consists of any ball that travels completely through the batter's box between the ground and the top of the batter's head, if the ball is not hit.

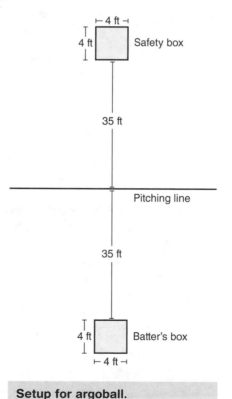

Setup for argoball.

- ► Regardless of whether the ball is hit or not, the batter must leave the batter's box, run to and place at least one foot in the safety box, and run back, placing at least one foot in the batter's box without getting tagged by a defender in order to score a 1-point run.
- ► A batter can wait in the safety box while the next batter bats but must run immediately if the ball is hit or missed.

► Every player on a team takes one turn at bat before switching from offense to defense.

► An out occurs if a fly ball is caught before it hits the ground, or if the batter is tagged with the ball by a defensive player as the batter runs to and from the safety box.

VARIATIONS

► Change the distance between the boxes.

► Change the size of the boxes.

For a complete description of this game and its modifications, see Todorovich et al. (2008).

Todorovich et al., 2008

Baseketball

PLAYERS

4 players per side

EQUIPMENT

3 buckets, plastic cricket bat, small Gator Skin ball, 6 poly spots

ORGANIZATION

For this game, place three large buckets in a triangle about 20 feet (6 m) apart. Between these bins place five poly spots evenly spaced. Finally, set a sixth poly spot to act as a home base about 15 feet (4.5 m) from the first and fifth.

RULES

► The batter receives an underhand toss from a pitcher who is on the same team. The batter must hit the ball forward, and it must travel past at least the first two poly spots.

► Once the ball is hit, the defense must get the ball into one of the three buckets in order to freeze the runner.

► The pitcher is allowed to defend the buckets after the ball is put in play. He cannot kick the ball or touch the ball before the defense has possession of it. Once the defense has possession, the pitcher can try to prevent the defense from scoring a basket but cannot foul or strip the ball.

► A batter is out if

– the ball is caught before bouncing or after one bounce,

– the ball does not travel past the hitting line,

– the defense gets the ball into a bucket while a player is not on a base, or

– the pitcher makes contact with the hit ball or fouls a fielding player.

► Teams change roles after two outs.

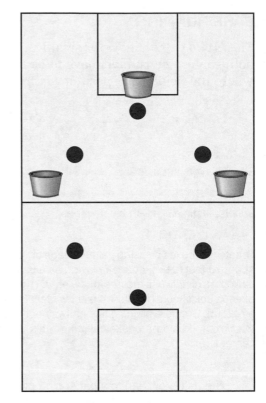

Setup for baseketball.

VARIATIONS

▶ Change location of poly spots.

▶ Change the required task for the fielding team to stop runners.

Poor Striking and Fielding Games

Given cricket games can last five days, and there are only two batsmen at any one time, it is not surprising that many top-level players are also expert card players. From a fielding perspective, we are also aware of the potential for players to be stuck in the outfield, either by choice, or worse, having been sent there by their teammates. By their very nature, striking and fielding games do have significant potential for considerable inactivity.

When designing games in this category, students need to be aware of situations in which waiting may occur and try to make alternate rules, or at least keep waiting to a minimum. Consider circle smash. In its first draft the game was played five versus five. However, even though each batter's turn might take only a minute, playing the game as individual batters means no one is waiting at all.

Striking and fielding games in which the pitcher dominates also have the potential for a lot of inactivity by the fielding team. If batters cannot put the ball in play, there is no need for any defense. Likewise, in the case of softball and baseball, if the pitcher is weak and walks most batters, there is again the potential for extended periods in which the fielders will not be involved in the game. Designing games where batters receive a pitch from one of their teammates can help solve this problem.

Safety in Striking and Fielding Games

Safety is an important issue in all game forms, and striking and fielding games are no different. Three areas need to be considered for safe play: (1) the playing area itself, (2) protection for the batting team, and (3) protection for the fielding team.

ENSURING A SAFE PLAYING AREA

In striking and fielding games, a lot of the action takes place at ground level. Batters are running and turning, fielders are moving to intercept balls, and in many situations, the balls are often traveling quickly on the ground. Consequently, the play area should be as smooth and level as possible. Fields should be free from holes, damage, stones, glass, and other foreign objects. Players need to be confident they can run, change direction, and even slide without the risk of turning an ankle or twisting a knee as a result of stepping in a hole. They also need to be confident that they can bend down to field a fast ball without it suddenly rearing up and hitting them in the face.

PROTECTING THE BATTER

In games where the ball is hard and will be traveling quickly, batters should wear approved protective helmets during batting practice as well as during games. It should be noted that all of the games presented in this chapter would not require such gear, but that does not preclude students from designing games in which such protection is necessary. In either case, games designers should be cognizant of the need to protect the batter.

Safety issues apply not just to the batters. Members of the batting team need to be positioned in safe places to avoid being hit with either the ball or the bat if it is let go by the batter during a hit. Dugouts and other waiting areas should be positioned well behind the firing range of the batter. In addition, during practice and games, all players should be alert and watching the batter on each pitch.

PROTECTING THE FIELDERS

Players on the fielding team need protection commensurate with the type of ball being used. In cases where the ball is hard and will be traveling at speed, the need for a fielding glove will be a question for games makers. Although not all players may need a glove, certainly those in key positions, such as those receiving a pitch (e.g., wicket keepers and catchers) will need protection for the hands and head area.

Questions to Consider When Designing Striking and Fielding Games

When designing invasion games, it is possible to start planning from a number of different perspectives (e.g., how to score, what equipment to use, how to move the ball). In striking and fielding games, however, it is more manageable to follow a particular design sequence. This section lists the questions that need to be answered by games makers when they create a striking and fielding game.

- **How do you score?** Scoring in striking and fielding games can be achieved in three ways. These include (1) hitting the ball past a certain point, (2) running past a certain point, and (3) running a particular pathway. Of course, games can include more than one of these, and there can also be multiple options within each of these. For example, in over-the-line Wiffle ball, the batter can score doubles and home runs, but other games may have many lines with different scoring values. Likewise, there can be different areas toward which to run that can have different point values. The higher-risk options will most likely have a higher point value. Pathways too can be manipulated to include any number of bases.

- **How do you get out?** There are a large number of options available for getting out. These are divided into situations when the player is batting or when she is running between bases. The most common forms of out for batters are (1) being caught, (2) after taking a specific number of unsuccessful swing attempts, and (3) having the pitch or bowl hit a target. In cricket they have developed 10 ways of getting out. These include deliberately obstructing the fielder, blocking the pathway to the wicket, and hitting the ball away from the wicket. Double hits are also banned from most games so that players cannot "set themselves up" for a better shot.

With regard to catching, some games allow for a batter to be out if the ball is caught after one bounce. To make this more of a challenge, that catch is often required to be with only one hand. From a strategic (and hence fun) perspective, this rule allows the fielding team to move in closer to the batter, encouraging the batter to hit the ball over their heads. However, this lofted hit provides the fielders with the opportunity of turning and making a running catch with one hand. When playing indoors, decisions have to be made about catching the ball off the wall. Again, some game forms require a one-hand catch off the wall or ceiling, but this is not cast in stone.

Many striking and fielding games will also include outs for players after a certain number of swing attempts. However, in the name of inclusion, more effective games have some other option for batters. The most common is moving to a particular point from which the batter then becomes a base runner for the next batter. Then on the next contact, both players become runners. Sometimes teams will choose to send multiple players to this "waiting base" from where they all run when the big hitter is at bat.

An alternative to the limited swings rule is the inclusion of a target, which if hit, puts the batter out. Usually in these games, the batter does not have to run if he hits the ball, unlike the swing rules mentioned already. If using a target, games planners need to decide upon the size, shape, and location of the target, together with compulsory or voluntary running rules.

Once the ball is hit, most striking and fielding games will involve base running. The most common options for dismissing a runner are (1) getting the ball to the base before the runner, (2) tagging the runner with the ball when she is off a base, and (3) hitting the runner with the ball when she is off a base. If required base-running zones are included (as in softball), additional consideration needs to be made of the consequences of running out of this zone. Finally, decisions need to be made as to whether the runner can disrupt the fielders in their quest to catch or collect the ball. Although all traditional striking and fielding games do not allow for obstructing the fielders, the freedom inherent in games making does not preclude some form of fielding disruption by the batting team (see baseketball, page 110).

- **What implements will be used?** Striking and fielding games all involve an object to be hit and something to hit it with. Most common are long-handled bats and small balls, but this is limited only by tradition. Other options for striking include using the hand or foot to send the ball into play, short-handled objects such as paddles, or large-handled objects with big hitting surfaces such as rackets. The choice of ball is usually determined following the choice of bat, as these pairings are interdependent. That is, certain balls are unsuitable for certain bats but very appropriate for others. Consider a playground ball. It would be difficult to generate any force on the ball using a small paddle but very easy when kicking the ball into play.

- **How does the batter receive the ball?** In most traditional striking and fielding games the batter receives the initial delivery from the fielding team, but this does not have to be the case. For example, in many children's games a tee or machine is used to provide a more predictable pitch. Alternatively, batting teams can use their own players to pitch. This usually results in more balls being put into play, as the batter can choose the pace and location of the incoming ball. Some batters might prefer a low pitch; others may rather swing at a higher

Pitch to your own team.

one. Still others might prefer the ball to have bounced first. The other advantage of same-team pitching is that the number of allowed pitches can be sharply reduced. That is, if you know exactly where the ball is coming from, you should need fewer attempts to hit it. Such games often allow only two swing attempts. Other alternatives include bigger balls or bigger bats with a larger surface area, or even cases where the batters can choose between bigger or smaller bats and bigger or smaller balls.

● **Where do batters hit from?** As mentioned, most striking and fielding games are played on fan-shaped or oval fields. In fan-shaped fields, there is no play behind the batter, and the batter always receives the ball from one space (as in baseball). In games played on an oval, where hitting can be in any direction, there are usually two batters with two hitting targets. Games designers will need to decide whether the batter will be hitting forward, hitting within a specific space, or hitting anywhere on the field, coupled with the original position of the batter in relation to the field dimensions.

● **What is the shape of the field, and what are the boundaries?** One attraction of striking and fielding games is that there is an unlimited shape of the playing area and little need for specific boundaries. All that needs to be determined is the fair and foul territories and any points to the batting team if the ball makes it to the boundary.

● **When do teams change from batting to fielding?** Although the most common transition between batting and fielding is after a designated number of outs, this does not need to be the case. However, if that option *is* chosen, games designers will need to decide on that particular number. Other choices include (1) after a specific time, (2) after everyone has a turn batting, (3) after a designated number of batters, and (4) after a specific number of pitches. When using the time option, it is usual to have penalty points or deductions to the total score for each player who got out during the time.

A Template for Designing Striking and Fielding Games

Table 8.1 provides a template of decisions that can be given to games makers when they are about to design a striking and fielding game. In table 8.2 on page 116, the game of poly spot cricket is presented using the key design questions.

TABLE 8.1—Template for Designing Striking and Fielding Games

Design question	Options
How do you score?	Hit over boundary Run to or past a point Run a pathway
How do you get out?	Caught (what about off the wall?) Throw to base After a number of swings or attempts Tagged Obstructing fielders Hit with the ball Run out of area Bat out of area
What implements will be used?	Hand Foot Body Bat Paddle Racket
How does the batter receive the ball?	Pitch to own team Pitch to opposition Pitch from a machine Toss to himself Off a tee Off a bounce
Where do batters hit from?	From an end line hitting forward From two end lines From the middle of the field to anywhere From a corner
What is the shape of the field, and what are the boundaries?	Rectangle Fan Oval Boundaries or no? What about walls and ceilings?
When do teams change from batting to fielding?	Number of outs Time at bat After certain score After everyone bats After number of batters

From P. Hastie, 2010, *Student-Designed Games: Strategies for Promoting Creativity, Cooperation, and Skill Development* (Champaign, IL: Human Kinetics).

TABLE 8.2—Poly Spot Cricket

Design question	Solutions
How do you score?	Scoring is accomplished by running to various poly spots of differing value. For each poly spot reached safely, that score is added to the batter's total. Poly spots are placed on either side of the pitch and can also be behind the pitching target. The teams decide before play upon (1) the total number of poly spots, (2) their placement, and (3) the scoring value of each one. The poly spots farther from the batter (and those behind the target) are worth more than those that are close by. Whenever the batter hits the ball, she must run to any one of the poly spots. If the batter misses the ball, she cannot run. If the ball hits the batter's body, the batter may choose to run or not. However, the batter cannot deliberately play at the ball with her body (e.g., kick it away).
How do you get out?	A batter is out if the fielding team catches the ball before it bounces twice or if the pitcher hits the wicket. The pitcher does *not* have to wait until the batter is ready before throwing at the target. There are two pitchers and two batters (one of each at either end), and the ball can be thrown from whichever end the fielding team chooses.
What implements will be used?	The batters will use a long-handled flat bat such as a cricket bat. The ball used will be a tennis ball or rubber ball of similar size. Targets can be a set of cricket stumps or a similar target about 2-3 ft (.6-.9 m) high and about a 1 ft (.3 m) wide.
How does the batter receive the ball?	The batter receives an overhand throw from the pitcher, who is positioned level with the stumps at the other end of the pitch.
Where do batters hit from?	The batter stands in front to protect the target and to hit the ball. However, he can hit the ball from any position, provided it is thrown by a pitcher. That is, the batter cannot interfere with a ball being returned by the fielders to the pitcher.
What is the shape of the field, and what are the boundaries?	The field may be any shape, and there is no need for any boundaries.
When do teams change from batting to fielding?	When all the players on the batting team are out, the teams change over. The team winning the toss can decide to bat or field first. Players can decide upon how many innings will constitute a game.

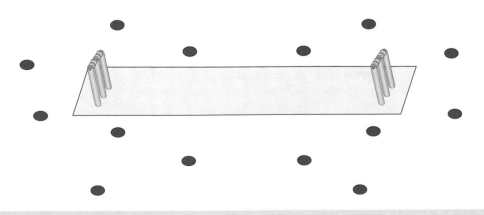

Setup for poly spot cricket.

Equipment for poly spot cricket.

Conclusion

Although traditional striking and fielding games involve long-handled implements and require batters to hit balls pitched to them at very fast speeds, it is
easy to construct games using small bats and friendly pitches. Further, games
designers need not be limited to playing games that use the familiar fan-shaped
field. Many over-the-line games have been introduced in this chapter that serve
to teach the key skills and strategies of batting and fielding roles.

Reference

Todorovich, J.R., Fox, J.P., Ryan, S., & Todorovich, S.W. (2008). A dynamic-rules game for
teaching striking-and-fielding game tactics. *Journal of Physical Education, Recreation &
Dance, 79* (5), 26-33.

CHAPTER 9

Net and Wall Games

Net and wall games are those where players take turns to send an object (usually a ball) back and forth over a net or to a wall. In games such as tennis and volleyball the players are separated by the net and occupy their own space, while in games such as racquetball and squash the playing space is shared. Although most net and wall games use rackets to strike the ball, this is not exclusive. For example, in volleyball the players use their hands, while in sepak takraw, a popular game in Southeast Asia, only the feet, knees, chest, and head are permitted contact with the ball.

As noted, it is not always a ball that is rallied in these games. Badminton is a familiar example where a shuttle is used rather than a ball, and in the social game of deck tennis, a rubber or rope ring is thrown over a net.

Key Principles of Net and Wall Games

No matter the form of net or wall game, the golden rule is that you must return the ball. Even if this return is feeble and nonthreatening, you are still alive in the rally, and there is the possibility your opponent will make a mistake. On the other hand, failure to return the ball instantly provides a point or a side-out to your opponent. If returning the ball is not problematic, the next strategy is to try to make your opponent struggle with his next shot. This can be achieved by either hitting the ball away from him or hitting to his weaker side (backhand or forehand) and then moving to intercept the return. If you are unable to make your shot irretrievable, you should aim to have your opponent hit the ball upward. A ball traveling up is far less threatening than a smash or a drive.

In net and wall games such as volleyball where multiple touches of the ball are permitted, it is possible to use those touches to first control the opponent's attack, then set up your own, and finally make a smash. In multiple-touch games, highly skilled teams or players are able to disguise their final attack, or at least make it difficult for the defenders to judge where and when the ball will cross the net.

Photo courtesy of Elliott Asbury.

In sepak takraw, you can contact the ball only with your feet, knees, chest, and head.

Required Experiences for Success in Net and Wall Games

To be a competent net and wall games player, students need experiences striking different sized balls with different sized implements. It should be recognized that striking becomes more difficult as the contact point gets farther from the body. Hitting with the hand is easier than hitting with a paddle, both of which are easier than hitting with a racket. For students practicing striking, initial experiences might include a slower ball or an enlarged racket head. It is possible to purchase slower traveling and less bouncy tennis balls, and a variety of badminton shuttles are available that travel at different speeds.

Net and wall games also place a great demand on one's agility. Games players should practice moving forward, backward, and side to side, both with and without the game implement. In addition, the correct hitting posture in each position should be practiced. For example, when running forward, the end position of the racket will usually be low (as in returning a drop shot), whereas when running backward, the end position will often be higher (as in preparing to hit an overhead shot). All of these agility drills should begin from the relevant base position appropriate to the game.

Players should also experience volleying, not just in the case of volleyball but also with rackets and smaller balls. Beginning tasks can include hitting continuously to a wall (with or without bounces), and later, hitting with a partner. Using walls is a great way to practice, even in games where the ball travels over a net. Individual and paired cooperative rallying should be a considerable part of the preparation for play in net and wall games.

Key Strategies for Success in Net and Wall Games

As mentioned previously, net and wall games involve a series of rallies where players move from offense to defense as the ball crosses the net or hits the wall. Ellis (1983) provides a useful model that conceptualizes a player's decision making off the ball and on the ball during a rally. An expanded version of this model is presented in figure 9.1.

THE FOUR RS

The first task during a rally is for each player to *read* the state of the game. Whether having just hit the ball or waiting for its return, questions that must quickly be processed include (1) where is the ball? (2) where is it traveling to? (3) where is my opponent? and (4) what subsequent options do I have? From the answers to these questions, the player will then *respond* with (1)

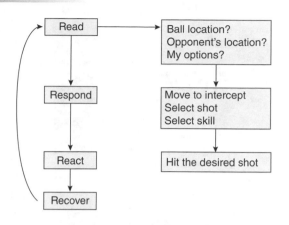

FIGURE 9.1 A player's sequence of decisions during a net game.

Adapted, by permission, from T. Hopper, 2003, "Four R's for tactical awareness: Applying game performance assessment in net/wall games," *Teaching Elementary Physical Education* 4 (2): 16-21.

a movement to intercept the ball, (2) a selection of the intended placement of the ball, and (3) a decision about the skill needed to achieve this shot. Following this off-the-ball stage, the player now must *react* to the pace and placement of the incoming ball and execute the desired shot. A *recovery* will follow where the player will attempt to get to the most appropriate court position to set up again for the *read* phase.

PROGRESSIONS OF OFFENSE AND DEFENSE

Like most games, net and wall games see players in both offensive and defensive positions. However, unlike invasion games when the team in possession is nearly always attacking while the team without is defending, in a net or wall game you can be defending when you are hitting or you can be on the offensive when it is your opponent's turn to hit.

When on offense, there are three progressions that players should follow in order. The first is simply to maintain the rally—as already noted, you must return the ball. There will be situations in rallies where due to the pace and placement of the opponent's shot, the only option you have is to hit the ball back in play. The second stage is to set up an attack. In this case you are able to hit the ball to spaces on the court in order to move your opponent left or right as well as forward or back. It is important to help players understand that at this point they need to be patient and not try to hit winners unless they are able to control the shot. In terms of consistency, accuracy should precede power. Players should also understand that the angle of a particular shot will often determine the angle of the return from the opponent.

Photo courtesy of Auburn University. Photographer Todd van Emst.

Stopping the ball from coming over the net.

The third stage of offense is winning the point. As noted earlier, if you can force your opponent to hit the ball in an upward direction, it is usually slower and allows you to get into position to spike or smash the ball downward.

From a defensive perspective, one's first challenge is to defend space. This will require a quick decision about where the ball is headed and a movement to get to that position. Although an attacking shot may not be possible from this position, at least the opponent will not achieve an outright winner. Part of this initial defense is returning to the central defensive position on court, anticipating where the next ball will be sent, and having an appreciation of the likely angle of that oncoming shot.

In some games, however, it is possible to actually defend against an attack. In team net games such as volleyball and sepak takraw, players are allowed to block an opponent's attack, by physically putting up some defensive wall to keep the ball from crossing the net.

Sample Net and Wall Games

The following set of games provides examples of the various configurations of net and wall games discussed to date. Wall ball focuses on space awareness and moving the opponent left and right, using catching as the primary skill. Long ball focuses on moving the opponents forward and back, as well as setting up an attack using volleying and spiking as the primary skills. Four square encourages players to stay in the rally by taking defensive or attacking options, while triangle mini tennis focuses on hitting accuracy and recognition of open spaces while striking with a paddle.

The game of tchoukball (Brandt, 1971) is also introduced as a team sport that focuses on sending the ball to open spaces. Tchoukball is unique in that there are two nets, and instead of sending the ball *over* the net, a team must bounce the ball off the net so their opponents cannot recover it.

Wall Ball

PLAYERS

2

EQUIPMENT

Gator Skin ball or a ball that is soft but will bounce, poly spots for boundaries

ORGANIZATION

Two players form a square or rectangle boundary against a wall. Players can decide upon the dimensions according to an agreed level of challenge. Players can also decide whether or not to include a line on the wall above which the ball must hit.

RULES

▶ Player 1 serves using an underhand volleyball serve against the wall.

▶ The other player can either catch the ball on the fly or let it bounce and then return it with a serve.

▶ If the ball lands out of bounds or a player cannot retrieve it after one bounce, a point is scored.

VARIATIONS

▶ Enlarge the court and allow two bounces.

▶ Play in a corner so two walls are in play (expand game to two versus two).

▶ Change to a pyramid ball—one that bounces randomly.

Long Ball

PLAYERS

2 players per side

EQUIPMENT

Large playground ball, 2 long jump ropes or floor tape to mark the center area

ORGANIZATION

Play is on a long narrow court (perhaps only 10 feet [3 m] wide) with no baseline.

A center area about 6 feet (1.8 m) is marked between the two half courts. A ball landing in this area is out of bounds.

RULES

▶ Play begins with a serve. One player bounces the ball and then hits it over the center space using one or two hands. Teams negotiate how far behind the center space the serve must begin.

▶ Each team has two touches and two bounces on its side.

▶ Contact can be with any part of the body.

▶ The ball must be struck or volleyed—it cannot be caught and thrown.

▶ The team winning a rally gets a point and the next serve.

▶ There is no baseline. The ball can be sent as far back as desired.

VARIATIONS

▶ Incorporate one side wall (where players develop rules for wall touches).

▶ Play three versus three, increasing touches and bounces.

Four Square

PLAYERS

4

EQUIPMENT

Large playground ball, 2 long jump ropes or floor tape to mark the center area

ORGANIZATION

Four square is played on a square court divided into four smaller squares of equal size. Usual size is 5 feet by 5 feet (1.5 m by 1.5 m) for each square.

RULES

▶ The player in the top square begins the game by serving the ball to one of the other squares.

▶ Players allow the ball to bounce in their square once, and the occupant of that square must return the ball to any other player's square by hitting or striking the ball with the hands.

▶ Once the ball lands in a new player's square, that player must return it, and so forth, until a player makes an error.

▶ The player who made the error moves to the bottom square, and the remaining players advance into the open squares.

VARIATIONS

Players decide upon the following rule options:

▶ Whether volleying is permitted

▶ Whether hitting overhand (i.e., smashing the ball) is permitted

▶ How to serve

▶ Where to serve from

▶ Size of the court

▶ Balls landing on lines

Triangle Mini Tennis

PLAYERS

2

EQUIPMENT

Slow-bounce tennis ball, net, junior tennis rackets, poly spots or playground chalk

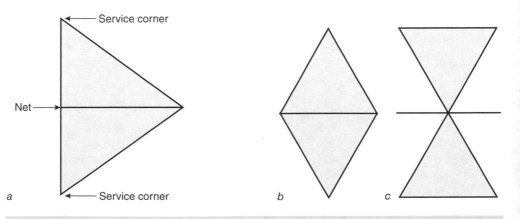

Basic setup for triangle mini tennis (a) and two possible variations of the basic setup (b, c).

ORGANIZATION

Place poly spots or use playground chalk to draw two triangles. The shape of the triangles is optional, but for starters, follow the diagram shown.

RULES

▶ The serve is underhand from a bounce. One player serves for five rallies and then they alternate.

▶ There is no volleying—the ball must bounce, but only once.

▶ The ball must be returned anywhere inside the opposing triangle.

VARIATIONS

Change the orientation of the triangle (e.g., apex at the end, base as the baseline, or apex as a baseline and base at the net).

Tchoukball

PLAYERS

9 players per side

EQUIPMENT

Two rebound frames, small firm ball (size 4 soccer ball or team handball), poly spots or floor tape to create the D-zone

ORGANIZATION

A regular court measures 130 feet by 65 feet (65 m by 20 m), but this can be modified for developmental appropriateness and player number. One rebound frame is placed at each end of the field. In front of each frame, a semicircle (usually 10 feet [3 m] in radius, but modifiable) defines a forbidden zone.

RULES

▶ Each team can score on both ends of the court.

▶ In order to score a point, a player must bounce the ball off the frame such that no defending player can catch it before it falls on the field of play.

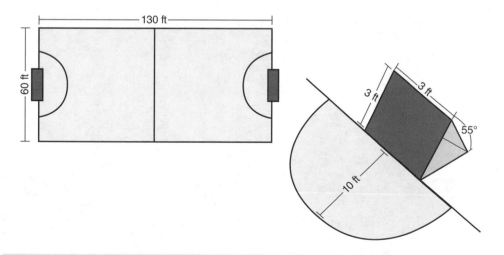

Tchoukball court and goal area.

▶ Physical contact is prohibited.

▶ A maximum of three passes is allowed to put one player in a position to shoot. Defending players are not allowed to interfere with this preparation, but they must anticipate in order not to be surprised by the ball's trajectory when it bounces from the frame.

▶ Control of the ball is handed to the other team after every shot at the frame or after every fault.

▶ Faults
  – touching the ball with the leg
  – taking more than three steps with the ball
  – holding the ball for more than three seconds
  – making more than three passes before a shot
  – dropping the ball
  – touching the ball rebounding from the net after a teammate's shot and the ball falls down into the field of play
  – making contact with the forbidden zone

▶ Scoring. A point is awarded if
  – the ball rebounding from the frame touches the field of play before a defender can catch it,
  – the ball rebounding from the frame touches a defender who fails to control it by dropping it on the floor or knocking it out of play,
  – a player shoots and misses the frame,
  – the ball rebounding from the net after a shot falls out of play or into the forbidden zone, or
  – a shot rebounds and hits the shooter.

▶ The team that has conceded a point restarts the game. The restart takes place behind the baseline and beside the frame on which the last point was scored.

▶ Following the restart, the first shot may be on either frame provided the ball has crossed the centerline of the playing area. The restart does not count as one of the three passes.

Photo courtesy of Francesca Castelli.

Tchoukball in action.

Poor Net and Wall Games

One of the major challenges when designing net and wall games is to avoid situations where a lot of people are waiting for turns or are not involved. Given most net and wall games are played in singles or doubles formats, it is important to make sure there are enough courts so that everyone can participate. We are all too familiar with the "too many players on a court" syndrome—such as eight- or nine-a-side volleyball. In fact, even six a side for novice volleyball players is too many to achieve a good game.

With regard to courts themselves, care must be taken not to create courts that are too large or too small. When the court is too big, rallies can be finished very quickly, resulting in time being spent chasing after loose balls. When the court is too small, players cannot adopt the key tactics of trying to move their opponents out of position. What often eventuates is a series of cooperative rallies where the ball is simply hit continuously back and forth across the net. Games designers will need ongoing experimentation with net heights and court dimensions in order to strike the best balance between games that have a reasonable degree of continuity but enough scope so that the more skillful and tactically astute players can come out on top.

Safety in Net and Wall Games

Although it may seem a little unexpected, I suffered my three most significant injuries while participating in net and wall games. One was a broken ankle during a volleyball game, another was bleeding into the eye during racquetball, while the third and perhaps most amusing was getting knocked out while playing table tennis! However, these three injuries highlight the main safety issues to be considered when playing net and wall games.

With wall games in particular, when players are sharing space there is potential for collisions between player and player, between player and walls, and between a player and the opponent's racket. Rules should be incorporated so that before they hit the ball, players know where their opponent is, where the ball is, and where they are in relation to both of these. If players do not know these locations, they should be required to stop playing and say, "Sorry, but I wasn't sure where you were and didn't want to swing." Rules should also be included that require players to get out of the way of their opponent's shots.

Any rackets or paddles that are used should have a good grip and if necessary a safety strap so they do not fly out of the hands of those playing. The balls in indoor wall games also can travel at great speed. If this is the case in a designed game, appropriate eyewear is recommended.

Although one is unlikely to be hurt if struck by a table tennis ball, in many net and wall games players are moving backward or toward the sidelines. The playing area should subsequently be free of hazards such as equipment, furniture, or exposed beams in corners or on sidelines. My concussion was the result of running backward into a pillar underneath a school building while playing table tennis. Play areas also need surfaces that are smooth, level, and dry. The poles used in net games may need to be padded if players are likely to run into them.

As mentioned in the section on poor invasion games, using many courts is one way to overcome low levels of participation. We need to be particularly conscious of the spacing between courts so that players are not running across the pathways of other games. There is also a need to put in place specific safety rules for when balls from one court roll onto another. There have been some very nasty injuries in volleyball when players have landed on a loose ball.

Questions to Consider When Designing Net and Wall Games

Although net and wall games are relatively simple in terms of the need for elaborate equipment and sophisticated rules, simply asking students to "make up a net game" can still leave them with insufficient resources to create a quality activity. This section lists the questions that need to be answered by games makers when they create a net or wall game.

● **How many players?** Although most net and wall games are played either as singles or doubles contests, this is not exclusively the case. Volleyball, for example, is played with six on each side in its adult form. Games makers should experiment with team net games to determine the best playing number.

● **How do you score?** Although in invasion games there are numerous ways to score, in nearly all net and wall games a player scores if the opponent cannot return the ball. This failure to return may include missing the ball altogether, hitting it out of bounds, or failing to get it over the net or to the wall. Other components of scoring will include the legality of the hit. As noted, many net and wall games use different rackets or body parts to strike the ball, and points may be awarded for infractions relating to their proper use.

A unique feature of net and wall games is the rally. Consequently, a key scoring decision will be whether to award a point to the winner or each rally (no matter who served) or to award points only to the serving team. In the second case, winning a rally when not serving will result in no points but the right to serve.

● **Where does the ball travel?** Designers of net and wall games do have considerable flexibility about the possible pathways of the ball. For net games, the ball might travel over a net or over a line. Where nets are not available, it is possible to divide the court into two halves, with a space in between that is considered out of bounds.

In some wall games such as squash, the ball must hit the wall above a baseline but below an upper limit. Still, in other games such as racquetball there are no such limits. If using walls or ceilings, decisions will need to be made about whether the ball can hit the side walls, and if so, can it hit these side walls before hitting the front wall. In addition, the question of how many total wall contacts are allowed needs to be answered. Likewise, designers of net games will need to decide the outcome if the ball hits the net and goes over. This decision may be different on a serve or during a rally.

● **How many touches or bounces are allowed?** Games designers will also need to make decisions about the number of touches each player or team has

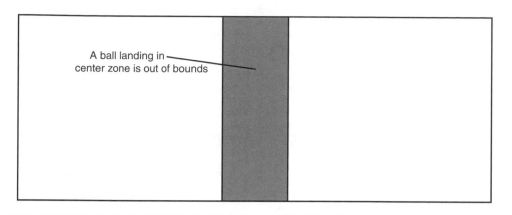

A ball landing in center zone is out of bounds

Use tape to create a center zone instead of a net.

on the ball, as well as how many bounces are allowed. In table tennis and rac-quetball, players are limited to only one touch and one bounce. In volleyball, no bounces are allowed, but a team has up to three touches to get the ball over the net. This combination of touches and bounces needs to be taken into account. Increasing both touches and bounces increases the repertoire of strategies and the diversity of skills available in a game. In addition, allowing for more touches and bounces can accommodate more players, as these games will often be played on larger courts.

• **What implements are used?** In net and wall games, the most common implements used are short-handled paddles and long-handled rackets. The body parts most commonly used in striking include the hands, arms, feet, and head. No matter the implement chosen, most games will provide limits on the legality of its use. Net and wall games do not however have to be striking games. It is perfectly reasonable to throw an object over a net (either overhand or underhand) or to a wall. In jai alai, for example, players wear a basketlike device called a cesta that is strapped to the right hand to hurl a hard rubber ball toward a wall.

Photo courtesy of Angel Gamarra.

Jai alai offers a different way of sending an object.

• **What type of ball or object is used?** Most net and wall games will involve rallying a ball. The ball may be large and inflated like a beach ball or may be as small and compact as a squash ball. Games designers need to experiment with a number of balls while understanding that the size and density of a ball will affect its speed and, ultimately, its ability to be controlled. Balls that are larger and lighter will result in longer rallies as they travel more slowly, while smaller balls will usually travel faster.

There is no rule in games making, however, that mandates a round ball be used. The badminton shuttle and the deck tennis ring have already been mentioned as alternatives. However, there is nothing to stop games designers using Frisbees, oval-shaped or pyramid balls, or any piece of equipment that provides good flight.

• **How does the game or rally start?** Net and wall games have a common starting point—the serve. This serve can be a tossed ball as in tennis or a shuttle hit underhand as in badminton. The ball may be bounced and hit (e.g., pickleball), thrown (e.g., deck tennis), or kicked (e.g., sepak takraw) over the net. In some net and wall games the rules indicate specific places where the serve must land to be legal. In these games, courts are lined to designate these areas. In wall games such as racquetball, squash, and jai alai, the serve must rebound off the wall and past a specific line.

• **What are the court dimensions?** With regard to court dimensions, games designers need to decide upon the height of the net, or if a wall is being used, the height of any lines on the front and side walls. Nets that are higher will cause rallies to be longer as there are fewer opportunities to spike or smash. If walls are in place, the height and length of the sidelines and end lines will need to be considered (if these are necessary at all). In some team wall games, there is no need for an end line as players can distribute themselves in cases where there are multiple bounces and touches allowed.

Photo courtesy of David Small.

The jai alai court has only one side wall, and it is 176 feet (54 m) long!

- **After a rally?** At the end of a rally, a rule will be needed about how to resume play. Does the winner get to serve, or perhaps the loser? In some games such as table tennis, the same player or team will serve for a specific number of points. In other games, to speed up play, an outside official will throw the ball into play (either to the winning or losing team), and the toss can be thrown anywhere on the court.

- **What other faults or penalties are included?** Faults and penalties in net and wall games typically relate to illegal use of a body part to contact the ball, or to the illegal use of the implement, such as a scoop or throw. The other major faults concern serving.

A Template for Designing Net and Wall Games

Table 9.1 provides a template of decisions that can be given to games makers when they are about to design a net or wall game. In table 9.2 on page 133, the game of over or under ball is presented using the key design questions.

TABLE 9.1—Template for Designing Net and Wall Games	
Design question	**Options**
How many players?	Singles
	Doubles
	Teams (number on each side)
How do you score?	Opponent misses ball
	Hit out of bounds
	Hit is not retrieved
	Rule infraction
	(Rally scoring?)
	(Score only on the serve?)
Where does the ball travel?	Over a net
	Over a line
	Across a space
	Above a line on a wall
	Within a boundary
	(Net? Wall?)
	(Double wall?)
What implements are used?	Paddle
	Racket
	Hand
	Foot
	Head
	Arms

From P. Hastie, 2010, *Student-Designed Games: Strategies for Promoting Creativity, Cooperation, and Skill Development* (Champaign, IL: Human Kinetics).

(continued)

TABLE 9.1   *(continued)*

Design question	Options
What type of ball or object is used?	Size of the ball Inflation of the ball Density of the ball Shuttle Frisbee Ring Other object
How many touches or bounces are allowed?	One touch Limited touches Infinite touches No bounces Limited bounces Unlimited bounces
How does the game or rally start?	Serve Volley Strike Toss to either side
What are the dimensions?	Length of sidelines Width of end lines No sides or ends Net or wall (or combination) Net height Lines on walls How many walls
After a rally?	Winner gets serve Loser gets serve Toss ball in Set number of serves
What other faults or penalties are included?	Service error • foot fault • serve to wrong area • illegal serve action • hitting the net • illegal use of racket or body part • interference

From P. Hastie, 2010, *Student-Designed Games: Strategies for Promoting Creativity, Cooperation, and Skill Development* (Champaign, IL: Human Kinetics).

TABLE 9.2—Over or Under Ball

Design question	Solution
How many players?	The game can be played in a 2 vs. 2 or 3 vs. 3 format.
How do you score?	A point is scored each time the receiving team fails to get the ball back to the opponent's court. This may include (1) if the ball does not go over the net or the lower obstacle, (2) if it lands out of bounds, (3) if it lands on the receiving team's court after traveling over the net, (4) if the receiving team catches an "over" throw with two hands, or (5) if the ball bounces twice after an "under" throw. A point is awarded for each rally, and the winner is the first to reach 21.
Where does the ball travel?	Play is on a badminton court, using a badminton net and a lower net made of traffic cones, benches, or some other obstacle. There are two possible flight paths for the ball. The first is over the net, while the second is below the bottom of the net but above the obstacles.
What implements are used?	The ball is thrown, volleyed, or caught with the hands. The ball may be parried or juggled, but a player cannot use the body to support or trap the ball when trying to catch it.
What type of ball or object is used?	The ball used is a large reaction ball (8 in.; 20 cm) or a Catch-Ball (an inflatable ball with a 3 in. [8 cm] diameter center core with 6 soft spokes that are 4.5 in. [11 cm] long).
How many touches or bounces are allowed?	A ball traveling *over* the net must be caught with one hand before it lands. A ball traveling between the obstacle and the net can bounce once and may be caught with both hands. The return from a two-hand catch must be with one hand. The ball may be volleyed, but only with an underhand motion.
How does the game or rally start?	Play begins with a serve from behind the service line of the court. The serve must be an underhand throw over the net. Any player on the opposite side can receive a serve. The return of serve must also go over the net, following which any open space (i.e., over or under) can be used.
What are the dimensions?	Play takes place on a badminton court. The widest and longest lines on the court are used. The height of the net will be around 5 ft (1.5 m). The height of the lower obstacle can depend upon available resources and experimentation. As a good starting point, an obstacle about 2 ft (.6 m) in height works.
After a rally?	The winning team from each rally will take the next serve. Players on each side serve in turn. Players can decide if the same server continues until a loss of serve, or whether to alternate each time.
What other faults or penalties are included?	When required to catch with one hand (i.e., when the ball travels over the net), a receiver can use alternate hands to catch but not both at one time.

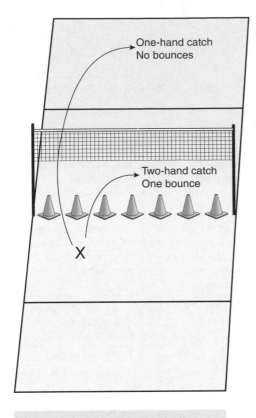

One-hand catch
No bounces

Two-hand catch
One bounce

X

Court for over or under ball.

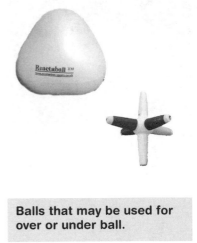

Balls that may be used for over or under ball.

Conclusion

Although most net and wall games involve only two players, this should not preclude games designers from thinking of games that have larger numbers on each side. Although two-player games can involve a number of different implements used to send the ball over a net, larger-sided games usually involve throwing and catching or volleying. Introducing students to games that cross an open space rather than a net will help them become more creative in their game design.

References

Brandt, H. (1971). Tchoukball: The sport of tomorrow! Edition Roulet, Geneva. Available: www.tchoukballpromo.com/general.html.

Ellis, M. (1983). *Similarities and differences in games: A system for classification*: Paper presented at the AIESEP conference, Rome, Italy.

Hopper, T. (2003). Four R's for tactical awareness: Applying game performance assessment in net/wall games. Teaching Elementary Physical Education, 4 (2), 16-21.

Moving Beyond Basic Games

- Apply games-making principles learned in part II to nontraditional game forms.
- Learn guidelines for assessing students and student-designed games.

Famous chefs tend to think of dessert as a counterpoint to the meal in which you play with different textures, colors, and flavors. Barbara Kafka for example, describes the dessert as a time to change the pace. You've had the pleasure of the dinner, and now you want another, different pleasure.

Part III of this book presents that change of color and texture. Here we explore games that force us to think out of the box. Chapter 10 introduces *conversion games*, games in which designers take elements from different game forms and morph them together to create totally original editions. Chapter 11 also takes a different path. In developing *cooperative games*, the focus is not on defeating an opponent but on achieving a particular outcome than can result only when all players use cooperative behavior and select strategies by a consensus decision-making process.

Finally, chapter 12 wraps up the book with an examination of how we can assess students and evaluate games. Several rubrics are presented that can be used to help students be more aware of their responsibilities *during* the games-making process, as well as to judge the quality of the games they have created.

CHAPTER 10

Conversion Games

The past five chapters have examined games that belong to a single category. That is, all the games in each category have a common tactical thread. In net games, the goal is to hit an object over a net so an opponent cannot return it. In invasion games, the common goal is to gain possession of some object, move it upfield, and then score by sending that object to a designated point. In this chapter, we will examine games that have been called *conversion games*. The definition of *conversion* has been kept quite loose, but in essence, the aim of these games is to extend students' thinking beyond the design templates that have been introduced in chapters 5 through 9.

De Sanchez (1995) has described two kinds of thinking. The first is called *incidental thinking* and emerges as a result of spontaneous and incidental contact with the environment. Examples from games making usually occur during the experimental phase of game play and might include how to deal with an out-of-bounds rule in an invasion or a tag game, or issues related to how long a player can remain in possession of a ball. *Deliberate thinking*, on the other hand, is the result of planned and carefully controlled thinking–learning processes. This is where students must stop and reexamine their games, either because something is not working or because they want to introduce a new avenue for scoring.

Although games making certainly presents a learning environment that De Sanchez suggests promotes thoughtful decision-making skills and opportunities, the design of conversion games takes this deliberate thinking to a new level. Examples of three types of conversion games will be presented in this chapter:

1. Hybrid games. Games that incorporate elements of two (or more) game forms (e.g., a combination of an invasion game and a target game).
2. Relocation games. Games that are reshaped to be played on different surfaces (e.g., modifying a game that was originally played on an outdoor court so it can be played in a swimming pool).
3. Transformation games. Games that use the same equipment but change the primary rules from one game form to another (e.g., changing a net or wall game to an invasion game).

These advanced games challenge experienced games makers in a number of ways. First, they require games players to have a good understanding of how games work. Without a sophisticated knowledge of the key principles of games, it is difficult to make alterations or additions to games that make them playable. Second, they stretch the imagination of games designers because there are few limitations with regard to following a script. Third, they present immediate problems that need to be solved, particularly with regard to the use and adaptation of equipment. The remainder of this chapter will provide samples of a number of conversion games and will also provide stimulus questions for teachers to help their students begin the process.

Hybrid Games

When designing hybrid games, students need to come to grips with the essential underlying tactical principles of the different game forms and see where they might be combined. Table 10.1 gives a summary of these key factors.

TABLE 10.1—Summary of Key Factors of Various Game Forms

Game form	Critical tactical issues	Essential manipulative skills
Tag games	• Fake the attack • Fake the defense • Keep distance from the tagger	• Throwing • Carrying • Catching
Target games	• Get close to the target • Block the opponent's target • Often self-paced	• Sending away
Invasion games	• Get possession • Move toward the goal • Score	• Catching • Trapping • Dribbling • Carrying • Sending away
Striking and fielding games	• Hit to spaces • Defend key spaces • Pitch to weakness • Swing or take • Run or stay	• Throwing • Striking • Collecting • Catching
Net and wall games	• Hit to spaces • Occupy key court positions	• Striking • Throwing

Ultimate Frisbee Golf

Ultimate Frisbee golf is a game that combines a *target* game (throwing a Frisbee to land in a target zone) with an *invasion* game (passing a Frisbee among teammates to move it into an end zone).

PLAYERS

5 players per side

EQUIPMENT

16 cones, 16 poly spots, Frisbee

ORGANIZATION

Near each of the four corners of a gym, create a square using four poly spots. The length of each side of these squares should be about one large step. These four corners act as the target "greens" for the golf version of the game. The tee boxes (of similar size to the greens) are made by placing four small cones in squares at the center of the court between each tee box. Two larger scoring zones (for touchdowns) are created using cones near the ends of the court, but in the center.

RULES

▶ Scoring can take place two ways:

1. Throwing the Frisbee from anywhere on the field to a teammate who catches it in an end zone, with both feet in the end zone (1 point).

2. Throwing the Frisbee from the tee box and onto a green. The throw from the tee box is an undefended shot and can slide, bounce, or fall onto the green for a score (3 or 5 points). A Frisbee must be at least halfway on a green to count.

▶ The first to 11 points wins the game.

▶ With the exception of a shot to a green, if a Frisbee touches the ground at any time, possession changes from the team who threw the Frisbee to the defending team.

▶ After any score (or missed attempt at a green), the other team gets possession. The players must throw the Frisbee past the throw-in line to score in the near end zone. A throw must take place. Running in the Frisbee will not be accepted.

▶ There is no out of bounds. The Frisbee can be played off of walls or other objects except the floor.

▶ Players should avoid physical contact with opponents.

VARIATION

Running with the Frisbee is allowed. In this case the following rule applies:

▶ If someone is tagged while she has possession of the Frisbee, she must immediately stop and make a pass.

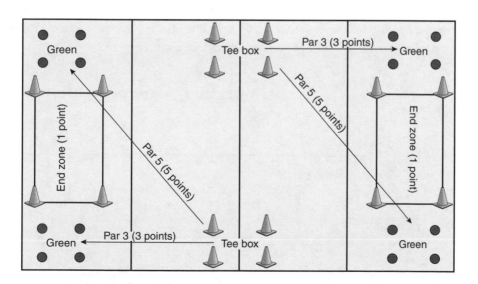

Setup for ultimate Frisbee golf.

Hoop Defense

Hoop defense uses the key principles of *target games* with an element of *striking and fielding* games. Although there is no actual striking in this game, what has been borrowed is the idea of alternate roles. In hoop defense, teams alternate trying to score as many points as possible while the opponent tries to score outs by limiting those options. As in a striking and fielding game, the two teams are doing different roles and try to match each other's score.

PLAYERS

4 (2 players per side), but can be expanded by any combination of 4

EQUIPMENT

6 hoops mounted on cones or poles, 2 stand-alone hoops, 2 Gator Balls or equivalent, poly spots or cones to act as the shooting line

ORGANIZATION

First, set up six hoop goals (hoops mounted on cones or short poles, placed evenly throughout the play area). Although it is preferable to have a wall behind these goals, it is not critical for the game. Create a shooting line and attacking zone using poly spots or cones. Place two balls within two hoops on the sides of the attacking area. As an estimate of the playing area size, approximate half of a volleyball court, with the back court as the target area and the front court as the attacking zone.

RULES

▶ Two balls start in the stand-alone hoops (one on each side of the space).

▶ Two players have 30 seconds to make two shots on any of the hoop targets.

▶ Different hoops are worth different points.

▶ For each ball, the pair has a maximum of three passes.

▶ Players can run with the ball.

▶ The defenders remain behind the shooting line and can defend any of the goals. Their challenge is to simply prevent a ball from going through.

▶ After the two shots (or if time expires), the attackers and defenders switch roles to complete the inning.

▶ If teams are four a side, the second pair from each team plays the second inning.

▶ Scoring can be for any designated amount of innings.

VARIATION

Both balls can be accessed by the attackers at the same time, but the players still have only three total passes.

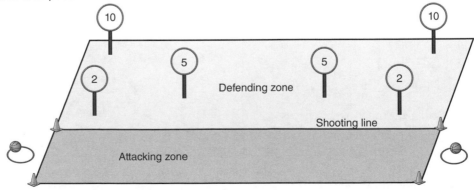

Setup for hoop defense.

Tenketball

Tenketball is a game that combines a *striking and fielding* game (hitting the ball to spaces to score runs) with a *target* game (sending a ball through a goal to score points).

PLAYERS

5 players per side

EQUIPMENT

1 cricket-type (flat) bat for the batter, 4 short-handled paddles for the fielders, 1 tennis ball, 2 large goals

ORGANIZATION

Set up two large goals about 10 feet (3 m) wide and 6 feet (1.8 m) high about 60 feet (18 m) apart. Field hockey goals are perfect here. If these are not available, you can use large cones and approximate some form of crossbar. Use field paint (or floor tape if playing indoors) to mark a running line about 3 feet (.9 m) in front of each goal.

RULES

- ▶ Bowler sends the ball to the batter, who can score two ways (players can negotiate the requirements of a legal pitch):
    - Hit the ball into the goal (4 points)
    - Hit the ball into space to make a run (1 point)
- ▶ The batter can be out three ways:
    - If the fielders volley the ball with their paddle and then catch it (can be caught by the same player or a teammate)
    - If the pitch enters in the goal (either by the batter's missing the pitch or a mishit into the goal)
    - If the fielding team sends the ball into the goal before the batter safely returns from a run (run-out)
- ▶ Fielders cannot throw the ball to return it but must hit it with the paddle.
- ▶ The ball must be hit into the goal by the fielders to effect a run-out.

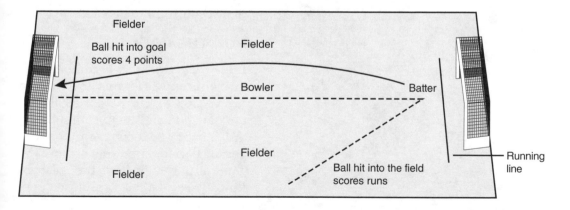

Setup for tenketball.

Relocation Games

There are a number of sports that can be played on different surfaces (e.g., natural or synthetic grass) or where the playing surface may change with the weather. Likewise, some sports are played both indoors and outdoors. For example, most formal basketball games are played on a wooden floor indoors, but there are many outdoor playgrounds around the world where games take place. In all these cases, however, the rules of these games remain exactly the same.

Conversely, when other games change from indoor to outdoor venues, many of the rules change. Teams of 11 contest soccer when it is played outdoors, while the indoor version is played in a 6-a-side format. In the indoor version, the playing area is bound by walls (like those used in ice hockey), and the ball may be struck in such a way that it contacts one or more walls without penalty or stoppage. Other differences include the type of ball, and in some leagues goals scored from a greater distance can be worth more points, similar to basketball. When played on sand, beach soccer is contested by teams of 5 with no offside rules.

Volleyball is another game that can be played on many surfaces. Indeed, there are tournaments for all-terrain volleyball in which teams compete indoors, outdoors on grass, and also outdoors on sand. Some versions of snow volleyball also exist. When moving a game between playing environments, it is important that the essential primary rules be kept intact. As a case in point, soccer in all its forms forbids the use of the hands and requires movement of the ball with only the feet and head to score a goal. Likewise, all volleyball games forbid the catching and throwing of the ball and allow multiple hits to send it over the net.

Table 10.2 provides examples of surfaces and locations in which transitions can occur. In this table, specific challenges are highlighted that result from the change.

RUN THE GAUNTLET

Run the gauntlet is a combination invasion and tag game in which a team scores by progressing a ball into an end zone and then running with a flag back to its own zone without getting tagged. First we'll explore the game as played on land, then discuss how it was adapted to play in a pool environment.

Photo courtesy of Oleg Sinelnikov.

Soccer in the snow brings its own challenges.

TABLE 10.2—Challenges Provided by Changing Environments

Challenge	1	Environment	2	Challenge
Reduced space Obstacles	Indoor	----	Outdoor	Wind Sun Precipitation Open spaces
Danger in falling Faster travel of the ball Cannot dive	Hard surface	----	Sand	Movement speed reduced Jumping restricted Agility compromised Uneven travel
Quicker play More distance on the pass Ball travels after the pass	Hard surface	----	Water	Locomotion changes Water depth affects fitness Nonswimmers and weak swimmers cannot compete with elite swimmers Ball won't travel along the surface Ball stops almost dead in the water Two elements: water and air Ball is wet and slippery Hidden element under the water (for fouls)
Harder to induce movement of the ball (e.g., spin in cricket and tennis) Greater care needed when jumping and landing	Hardtop	----	Grass	Allows for sliding Reduces velocity of rolling ball Unevenness
No sliding	Hardtop	----	Ice	Sliding possible Skating ability Little friction to stop players or the ball
Less speed More control in the turn Two hands on the ball	Ground	----	Air (carried: e.g., bike, horse, person, wheelchair)	Increased speed Increased height Ability to ride New skills to combine (e.g., riding and hitting)

Run the Gauntlet

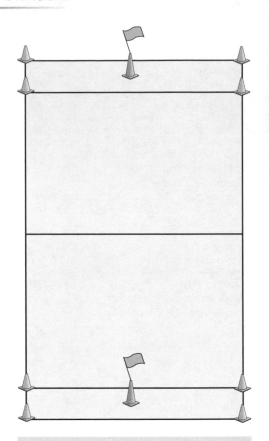

Setup for run the gauntlet.

PLAYERS

4 players per side

EQUIPMENT

8 cones to designate the scoring areas, Gator Skin ball or American football, 2 small dome cones with a short foam noodle or ball to designate a "flag" at each end of the pitch

ORGANIZATION

Set up a field of play about the size of a basketball court using four cones as end lines and a further four cones as the touchdown lines. In the center of each end zone place a small dome cone with a small section of a foam noodle (about 6 inches [15 cm] in length) on top of the cone. These act as the flags.

RULES

▶ The aim of the game is to get the opponent's "flag" and return it safely (without being hit by the ball) to your own end zone.

▶ Players must pass the ball between each other to move up the pitch.

▶ Players can run with the ball, but if they are touched then they must stop and pass. Taking three touches will result in a changeover of possession.

▶ If the ball is dropped then the other team can pick it up and attack. However, dropping the ball does not mean that there has to be a changeover, as the attacking team can also pick it up after they drop it.

▶ When an attacker succeeds in taking the ball inside the opposition's area, he may take the flag, but he has to leave the ball behind. After taking the flag, the attacker becomes a target as he attempts to run with the flag back behind his own end zone.

▶ To stop a player from scoring, the team who has had its flag taken must try to hit the player with the ball. Teams attempting to hit the flag runner can pass between each other, so think before slinging the ball anywhere.

▶ If the flag runner is hit with the ball, then the flag must be returned and the team that made the successful hit starts with a free pass from the edge of its scoring area.

VARIATION

▶ Allow the defending team to run with the ball until the halfway line.

▶ Have two cones at the halfway line. In this case, the touchdown scorer can attempt to steal the baseline cone for 3 points or one of the cones at half-court for 1 point.

When the designers of run the gauntlet took this game into the pool environment, a number of specific challenges arose. First, the dimensions of the game needed to be changed, as it was particularly difficult to delineate an end zone. Second, the pool had different depths at each end, so considerations of fairness had to be worked out. Third, the sponge ball that had been used in the outdoor game became waterlogged in the pool. Finally, once they captured the flag, smart players began to swim *underwater* with the foam noodle so that they could not be tagged.

The first three issues were easily addressed. Instead of an end zone, the target flag was replaced with a water polo ball on a cone placed on the edge of the pool. Second, the teams changed ends at halftime. In addition, it was decided that if a team had weaker swimmers, they were able stay in the middle of the pool when their team was in the deep end. However, they were not able to take the ball from the swim-off. Third, the sponge ball was replaced with a plastic inflatable ball of equivalent size and shape.

The fourth issue required more lateral thinking. The teams decided to replace the foam noodle they used in the outdoor version with a water polo ball that was almost impossible to submerge. In that way, it made the submerged swimmer moot, as it was impossible to progress with the ball. In addition, after a series of games, it was also determined that the ball had to be controlled (i.e., kept within arm's length on the return to the flag), as players had begun to throw it upfield and swim after it.

The other rule changes were mostly cosmetic but included the following:

- To start the game we will have a swim-off instead of the throw-in that was used on land (the referee will place the ball in the middle).

A water polo ball replaced the flag in the water version of run the gauntlet.

The water polo ball could not be submerged to prevent the target from being inaccessible.

- Rebounds off the side walls mean play on.
- Referees will not be in the pool as they can see better from the sides.
- Fouls are the same for bad language. However, pushing isn't going to make any difference underwater, so dunking or pulling on people's legs to hinder their swimming is classed as a foul instead.

PIKO PIKO

Piko piko is an invasion game that requires teams to score by throwing a ball from a plastic milk carton through a goal. When the players first took piko piko into the swimming pool, the tennis ball plugged the milk carton, so it promptly filled with water. Throwing the ball from the jug—the essential primary rule that could not be changed, suddenly became very difficult. As a remedy, holes were cut in the bottom of the milk containers to let the water drain out.

In addition, as the pool contained both deep and shallow ends, the students decided to make the deep-end goal smaller than the shallow-end goal to allow for the relative ease of defending the shallow end. The side hoops were also set back from the side and required an upward shot, and goalkeepers could not shoot.

Transformation Games

In these games, the challenge is to reconfigure a game so that it changes from either an invasion game to a net or wall game, or perhaps from a striking and fielding game to an invasion game. The limitations are usually that no new equipment can be introduced for the new game, but cones or markers can be used to delineate the playing space if necessary.

Transformation games again ask the games designers to show their understanding of how various game forms work and to consider the key tactical features of each game form when making changes. Again, the reminder sheet shown in table 10.1 on page 138 might be a useful resource, as is shown in the following game.

FROM NET GAME TO INVASION GAME

A group of students have designed a three-a-side net game in which a large playground ball is sent over a space (rather than using a net). Each team is allowed two bounces and three touches on each side. No catching is permitted; the ball may only be volleyed. Serving is underhand from a serving line back from the court.

The players made three changes to transform this game to an invasion game. First, they placed one player from each team in each of the three zones (the two courts and the center area), with the center player becoming a rover (a player who can go into any of the zones). They then moved the corner cones to form goals at each end. Finally, while retaining the three-bounce, three-touch rule, the goal was to now pass the ball (catching was allowed) among teammates to score through the goal.

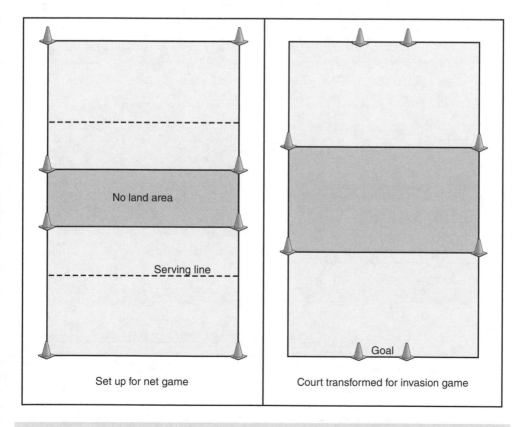

Set up for net game

Court transformed for invasion game

Changes in court alignment when transferring from a net to an invasion game.

FROM INVASION GAME TO TARGET GAME

A group of students have designed a three-a-side invasion game in which a Phlat Ball is passed between players in order to shoot at one of four cones placed on an end line. A Phlat Ball is a sports toy that transforms from a flying disc to a ball when it is thrown. Its variable time-delay feature provides a surprise transformation, so the player receiving the ball is not sure when it will change shape.

The player in possession cannot run or walk with the ball more than one pace, and contact with the ball carrier is penalized with a free pass. If the ball or player in possession touches or crosses the end line or sidelines, the opposing team gets possession from that point. After a score, the possession goes to the nonscoring team from that baseline. The cone that was knocked down is out of play, and the game continues until all four cones are knocked down or for a predetermined time limit.

The players made three changes to transform this game to a target game. First, they set up the cones in a diamond shape, similar to the orientation used in 10-pin bowling. They then lengthened the playing area. Each team took position on each end line and made alternate shots on the opponent's cones. The first team to knock down all four cones scored 1 point, and the cones were reset.

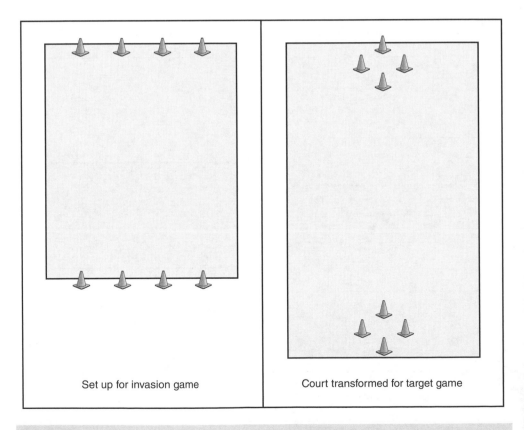

Set up for invasion game

Court transformed for target game

Changes in court alignment when transferring from an invasion game to a target game.

Conclusion

Although not part of the regular lexicon of games making, conversion games do give advanced students a chance to really challenge themselves, and they do enjoy the task of making combinations between various game forms. Nonetheless, these games require advanced tactical awareness, but when well developed, they can be exceptionally fun and exciting games. All that is required is a fertile imagination.

Reference

De Sanchez, M. (1995). Using critical thinking principles as a guide to college level instruction. *Teaching of Psychology, 22,* 72-74.

CHAPTER 11

Cooperative Games

In chapter 4 we describe games in which an opponent is either present (competitive games) or absent (noncompetitive games). Another way to conceptualize this difference comes from game theory (a field within economics) in which the two game types differ according to the *interdependence* among the players. In game theory, a competitive (or noncooperative game) includes significant details about all the rules and the moves available to the players. In a cooperative situation, the focus is only on the *outcomes* that result when the players come together in different combinations.

A cooperative game, then, is one where groups of players (often called *coalitions* rather than teams) must use cooperative behavior and select strategies by a consensus decision-making process. That is, in these games there is an enforced coordinated behavior on the members of the coalition. Simply, if coalition members do not make their contribution, the game cannot progress. Common to all cooperative games are situations where

- all players win or lose together;
- everyone plays;
- there are no traitors, scapegoats, false identities, or "one versus everyone else" situations; and
- preferably the games are not just multiplayer solitaire situations but require mutual reliance.

Many in physical education present a false dichotomy as a justification for cooperative games. We often see the following separation in which a "versus" approach is taken (table 11.1 on page 152).

If you closely examine the competitive side of the table, you can see the flaws in this argument. In the competitive games-making process, we don't eliminate players, the rules and strategies are developed to enhance the challenge and enjoyment of the game, and the essential goal is to encourage children to play a good game—one that is safe and inclusive, and where the offense and defense have an equal opportunity for success.

Likewise, the promotion of self-esteem and self-evaluation, as well as improving problem solving and decision making, are not the sole property of cooperative games. Moreover, cooperative games, when played well, do not always allow for

TABLE 11.1—Suggested Differences Between Cooperative and Competitive Games		
Cooperative games . . .	**vs.**	**Competitive games . . .**
encourage children to play with one another. allow everybody to win and succeed. eliminate fear of failure. let children play for play's sake. do not allow for elimination. are fun and supportive. build feelings of worth. increase self-esteem. are self-validating. encourage problem solving and decision making.		encourage children to play against one another. allow only half or one of the group to win. equate loss with failure. let children play to beat the other guy or girl. have frequent elimination. often have rules and strategies. are not always fun and supportive.

winning and success. Indeed, there may be times when students cannot achieve the preset goal of a cooperative game, and the lessons to be learned in these cases are often more valuable than those learned from success.

Adam Brandenburger (2007) from New York University's Stern School of Business sees the use of the terms *competitive* and *cooperative* as unfortunate. Brandenburger suggests that these terms "might suggest that there is no place for cooperation in the former and no place for conflict or competition in the latter." In fact he states that neither is the case and notes that "cooperative theory embodies not just cooperation among players, but also competition in a particularly strong, unfettered form."

Cooperative activities thereby involve competition, but the competition is usually with inanimate factors such as a challenge, a problem, time, quality of performance, or number of repetitions. As one group of my elementary students recently noted when playing blanketball, "We are playing against the net." To borrow again from economic game theory, we use the term *solution concept*. In game theory, a solution concept is a formal rule for predicting how the game will be played. These predictions are called solutions and describe which strategies will be adopted by players, therefore predicting the result of the game. Many solution concepts for many games will result in more than one solution, and each successive solution concept improves on its predecessor.

In his "Musings on cooperative game mechanics" on the BoardGameGeek Web site, Tim Deagan describes two types of scoring systems that relate to these solution concepts. The first is the personal-best (PB) scoring mechanism where you compare your score to your previous attempts. The second he calls the collapsing-ceiling (CC) model, which he likens to adventure movies where the protagonists are trapped in a room with the ceiling or walls closing in. In CC, you primarily want to survive, whereas in PB you want to maximize points. To put it simply, in cooperative games, the solution concept might include the following:

- See how many times
- See how many points
- See how long (or fast) it takes to complete
- See if you can complete the task

With each time the game is played, the players develop a more efficient method for completion.

Collective Scoring

Orlick (1977) suggests that *collective scoring* is the best term to be used when quantifying the challenge of a cooperative game. A collective is a group of people who share or are motivated by at least one common issue or interest, or work together on a specific project to achieve a common objective. In a cooperative game, two or more teams work together to achieve a solution to the game's challenge, and points are often called collective points, as teams do not achieve success at the expense of each other but rather as a result of working together.

The game of blanketball provides a good example of collective scoring. In blanketball, teams throw a ball back and forth over a volleyball net using only a blanket. Each successful catch scores a collective point. The game requires cooperation from all players *within* a team in order to control the ball and blanket, and it also requires cooperation *between* teams in order to send the ball over in a way it can be caught. Added challenge can be provided by replacing the blankets with towels and having two players holding each towel, one person at each end, but also by requiring a pass within a team before the ball is sent over the net. The term *cooperative interdependence* is used to describe situations such as this where the design of a piece of equipment forces players to work cooperatively to utilize it.

A second example of collective scoring and cooperative interdependence is the game of beach ball hoop. This game involves two pairs of players in which one set of partners is holding a hoop while the other pair (one on each side) attempts to volley a beach ball back and forth through the hoop. The hoop holders can move so that the beach ball travels through it. Again, there is cooperation *within* teams in that the hoop holders have to work together to manipulate the hoop, and cooperation must exist *across* the pairs to score collective points.

As is the case with blanketball, extra challenges can be included in beach ball hoop. Initially, a player may be allowed to volley the ball up to three times to send it through the hoop. Later, only one contact may be permissible. A second challenge might include players changing roles (from hoop holder to volleyer) without the ball touching the ground.

Beach ball hoop requires cooperative interdependence.

Reversal Games

Reversal games are those where players become members of both teams. Usually played with net games, as one player sends the ball over the net, he then quickly changes to become a member of the other team. The challenge is to keep a rally going until all players have switched sides. This pass-and-go format can be used in games such as volleyball, badminton, and table tennis.

Components of Cooperative Games

Orlick (1977) states that all cooperative games must have four basic components. These are cooperation, involvement, acceptance, and fun. Because many of your students will not have had experience with these cooperative components, it is suggested that you let them play a number of cooperative games and then discuss the goals of those games. In particular, time should be allocated after each game so the students can discuss the critical features of the game that required cooperation. In addition, you should ask ways in which the game provided for maximum involvement. Acceptance is more an attribute of how a group works together, while fun is usually related to the degree to which the challenge matches the skills of the participants: A good match usually means a game that is more fun.

Four sample cooperative games are provided to demonstrate how tag, net and wall, invasion, and striking and fielding games can be played in cooperative contexts.

Elbow Tag

One or more players are taggers, with an equal number of players being the runners. All other participants link elbows in either pairs or threes. The objective of the game is for taggers to chase and tag their designated runner, and if successful, they change roles. The runner, however, may link arms with either of the outside people in a pair or triad. When this happens, the person standing on the other side of the incoming runner peels off to become the new runner. The cooperative aspect of this game is that players are helping each other avoid the taggers.

Elbow tag.

Beat the Clock

Two teams of equal number begin on either side of a net. Their goal is to pass the ball (you decide what type of ball and the way it must be sent over) so that each player sends the ball over only one time. That is, if a player catches the ball a second time, he must pass to a teammate who has not thrown it over. Record the time taken to complete the task.

Box Soccer

In this game (described in Orlick 2006) four players stand inside a long jump rope that has its ends tied together. Beginning with the jump rope around the players' waists, the challenge is to keep the rope taut while passing and dribbling a soccer ball from one designated base to another, and hence score a collective point. Once the team delivers the ball to the next base, it then returns to the original base and collects the next ball, which has been placed there by another team. The game continues until each team's original ball is back where it started. The challenge is to reduce the time to score four points, or to see how many points can be scored in a designated time period.

Box soccer.

Jim's Rounders

In this striking and fielding game (named after Jim Deacove, a renowned cooperative games designer, and described in Orlick 2006), one team remains at bat until each person gets home. Players advance in the following manner. If they hit a ground ball, they earn one base. An infield fly earns two bases, while an outfield fly is a three-base hit. Runners advance as they would in softball or baseball. That is, a runner on first would move to third if the batter hits an infield fly. Teams can decide upon how many pitches a batter will receive and who will pitch to the batter (i.e., someone from the fielding team or a player from the batting team).

The cooperative element of this game is as follows. For a hit to count, the fielding team must stop a ground ball before it stops rolling or catch a fly ball before it hits the ground. That is, for the fielders to bat, they must work hard to stop the ball and make catches, while for the batters to score, they must hit *to* the fielders, and hit *soft* catches.

A Word on Sacrifices

In their text on team-building challenges, Midura and Glover (1995) introduce the notion of sacrifices. Sacrifices are penalties that are apportioned to teams if they break one of the rules of a game or challenge. The basis for including sacrifices is that occasional failure can actually build a stronger perception of eventual success. They also are designed to serve as specific points of accountability. That is, in the words of Midura and Glover, "sacrifices must be made if wrong responses occur. . . . we want participants to deal with more than just the direct consequences of errors. They must also deal with a sacrifice, having to give up something for their mistakes" (page ix). In team-building challenges, these sacrifices often include the elimination of players or a reduction in the number of options a team has to complete the task. However, within the context of games making and cooperative games in particular, the use of player elimination is less recommended. Nonetheless, there are many possibilities that games designers can include that increase the challenge without demeaning or excluding players.

A Template for Designing Cooperative Games

Table 11.2 provides a template of decisions that can be given to games makers when they are about to design a cooperative game. In table 11.3, the game of butterfly net (Omnikin, 2007) is presented using the key design questions.

TABLE 11.2—Template for Designing Cooperative Games

Game component	Questions
Coalitions (teams)	How many coalitions? How many players in each coalition? Any specific roles or restrictions within each coalition?
Scoring system	See how many times you can complete the task See how many collective points you can accumulate See how long (or fast) it takes to complete the task See if you can complete the task at all (any time limit?)
Equipment and resources	Equipment needed Playing space
Task details	What is the problem to be solved? What are players (all, or specific within a coalition) allowed to do? What specific restrictions are in place?
Sacrifices	Are there any sacrifices?

From P. Hastie, 2010, *Student-Designed Games: Strategies for Promoting Creativity, Cooperation, and Skill Development* (Champaign, IL: Human Kinetics).

TABLE 11.3—Butterfly Net

Game component	Solutions
Coalitions (teams)	The game is played by a coalition of four players who are working in pairs.
Scoring system	The objective is to make as many catches as possible before the ball is dropped. Each successful catch scores 1 collective point.
Equipment and resources	One hoop and one giant inflatable ball are required by each coalition.
Task details	Students pair up and share one hoop. The ball is placed within one hoop, and one player kicks the ball into the air. The second pair must catch the ball with the hoop before it hits the floor. Depending upon the playing area and skill of the participants, variations include playing off a wall or allowing one bounce.
Sacrifices	The pair receiving the ball must have both hands in contact with the hoop at all times. An optional sacrifice requires a player who lets go of the hoop to resume with hands crossed, or for a second infraction, to turn facing outward with her back to the hoop.

Butterfly net requires the use of a giant inflatable ball.

Possible increased challenges (sacrifices) for butterfly net.

Conclusion

Most competitive games involve the concept of zero sum, a situation in which a gain by one person or side is matched by a loss by another person or team. In cooperative games, however, players work together in order to achieve a goal, either winning or losing as a group. A further contrast between competitive and cooperative games is that these groups of players (known as coalitions) have the option of planning as a group in advance of choosing their actions.

References

Brandenburger, A. (January, 2007). Cooperative game theory: Characteristic functions, allocations, marginal contribution. Available: www.stern.nyu.edu/~abranden/teaching.html.

Deagan, T. (2006). Musings on cooperative game mechanics. Available: www.boardgamegeek.com/thread/100454.

Midura, D.W., & Glover, D.R. (1995). *More team building challenges*. Champaign, IL: Human Kinetics.

Omnikin. (2007). *Omnikin cooperative games manual*. Charny, Quebec: Omnikin.

Orlick, T. (1977). Cooperative games. *Journal of Physical Education & Recreation, 48* (7), 33-35.

Orlick, T. (2006). *Cooperative games and sports: Joyful activities for everyone*. Champaign, IL: Human Kinetics.

CHAPTER 12

Assessment in Student-Designed Games

Although a culture exists in many schools in which assessment becomes part of the educational reform agenda and is removed from student learning, the fundamental purpose of assessment is to allow teachers to gauge students' levels of understanding. From this point, the challenge is to make instructional decisions to help students develop knowledge and be motivated to learn (Melograno, 1997).

Any quality assessment scheme will entail three parts. These will include (1) determining what outcomes you would like to see from the unit of instruction, (2) selecting and then implementing appropriate measures to determine student progress toward meeting these outcomes, and (3) developing an evaluation scheme that provides direction to the program and whatever modifications can be made to increase both student and instructional success. It is the purpose of this chapter to provide some ideas and examples about what and how to assess in student-designed games.

What to Assess in Student-Designed Games

Planning for assessment begins with setting goals and asking questions about what you want to see from the students at the end of the unit. The global goals of student-designed games are for students to engage actively with and explore components of game play, to think critically about their experiences playing games, to learn how to learn cooperatively and solve problems in groups, and to create games that are meaningful to them as children while also focusing on significant skills and strategies of game play.

REQUIRED DISPOSITIONS

To achieve these goals, students will need to have certain dispositions and exhibit specific behaviors. These have been broken down into three groups: approach tendencies, personal and social responsibility, and knowledge.

Approach Tendencies   A student's approach tendencies are behaviors that he exhibits as he approaches a new topic, task, or area of study (Bocchino, 1999). Essentially, they are measures of attitude and can reflect either an approach or avoidance action. If someone has a positive or favorable attitude toward something (let's say participation in game play), we could expect him to take up opportunities that allow him to engage in it. Alternatively, if someone has a negative attitude toward something (let's say working in a group), then we would expect that he would avoid situations where he has to cooperate with others.

In student-designed games, we would hope students would have positive attitudes and hence favorable approach tendencies toward the following:

- Seeking opportunities to learn
- Practicing hard
- Accepting and acting on advice
- Participating enthusiastically

These would indicate that students are invested in the games-making process and thereby working toward achieving the long-term goals. Of course, not every class consists of strongly motivated and amenable students, and feedback relating to this is the first stage of creating change.

Personal and Social Responsibility   To effectively participate in the games-making process, students should also be competent with regard to a number of personal and social responsibility items. These include

- assuming responsibility for their designated roles(s) in the design and presentation of games;
- cooperating in a way that enhances class management;
- displaying tolerance for peers on an individual, team, and class level;
- exhibiting a commitment to the team; and
- playing fairly.

Demonstration of these characteristics would show that a student is contributing to the games-making process in a way that enhances not only her own learning but also that of others.

Knowledge   With regard to the knowledge-related aspects of games making, we should see evidence of students

- analyzing selected game-strategy problems;
- being able to develop solutions to game problems when they confront them;
- effectively explaining their own game to other students; and
- competently officiating and keeping score of their own game when others are playing it.

PERFORMANCE IN GAME PLAY

Although not a core feature of student-designed games, there is nonetheless some value in assessing students' performance in game play. After all, if we are expecting students to design good games, it would seem appropriate for us to measure the extent to which students can at least demonstrate some tactical awareness.

QUALITY OF GAMES

Although being cognizant of the idea that student-designed games are the property of their creators, it is still particularly worthwhile to give games designers feedback about their product. Having other students play their games and give their opinions allows for interaction between students, the sharing of ideas, and the opportunity for individual and group accountability. Recall that a key element of student-designed games is not simply telling students to "go make up a game." Receiving opinions and suggestions about how a game can be made fun, fair, and safe, and subsequently responding to these, is an essential component of the design process.

Sometimes games have to be radically redesigned following group feedback.

How to Assess Student-Designed Games

It is important to recall that student-designed games are more concerned with the process of games making rather than a particular specific outcome. Hence it is important that we focus on formative assessment. *Formative assessment* is a diagnostic use of assessment to provide feedback to teachers and students over the course of instruction. Feedback given as part of formative assessment helps learners become aware of any gaps that exist between their desired goal and their current knowledge, understanding, or skill and guides them through actions necessary to obtain the goal. In some countries, formative assessment is appropriately called assessment for learning.

The conditions for successful formative assessment are shown in figure 12.1.

This section will provide examples of assessment instruments that can be used to give students feedback about their attainment of the various goals of games making described in the previous section. All the forms are presented at the end of the chapter. Feel free to photocopy these for your use during games-making units.

MEASUREMENT OF DISPOSITIONS

The most common format of providing students with feedback about their performance on the various games-making dispositions is through the use of rating scales and checklists. Assessments 12.1, 12.2, and 12.3 (pages 168 to 170) provide sample checklists that you can use at various stages through a games-making unit. Although each uses a different scoring scale, the common aim among them is to give students some form of feedback about their progress.

1. The student and teacher share a common understanding of what constitutes quality work. That is, they have the same standards for achievement.

2. Both student and teacher can compare the student's performance to these standards.
   - The student assesses as he is working on the task at hand *and* upon completion.
   - The teacher may assess the completed work *or* while the work is in progress.

3. Following the assessment, teaching and learning activities are adjusted to close the gap between the student's performance and the standard.
   - The teacher not only assesses the student's performance but also provides feedback (guidance) to the student, enabling her to improve her performance.
   - The student will use what she has learned from the assessment to improve future performances.
   - The teacher also assesses the instruction that preceded the performance. The teacher will adjust instruction based on this assessment.

FIGURE 12.1 **Processes of formative assessment.**

MEASUREMENT OF PERFORMANCE DURING GAME PLAY

If your goal as teacher concerns students playing a good game, then your assessment must also center on game play. Although there are a number of instruments that are used to assess students' skill performance in isolated tests, the Game Performance Assessment Instrument (GPAI; Oslin, Mitchell, & Griffin, 1998) and the Team Sport Assessment Procedure (TSAP; Grehaigne, Richard, & Griffin, 2005) have proven popular in that they focus upon a player's performance within the context of a game.

The key difference between the two is that the GPAI measures not only skill execution but also decision making. This serves to make the instrument more comprehensive and perhaps more suited as an evaluation tool in student-designed games. However, given that it attempts to measure less observable attributes, the GPAI is at the same time more complex. Trying to make a judgment about a player's decision making is not easy and often requires sophisticated judgment by someone who understands games well.

The GPAI was designed to measure game performance behaviors by assessing a player's ability to select and apply appropriate skills. The GPAI provides analyses of individual game performance components such as decisions made, skill execution, and support as well as overall performance components such as game involvement and game performance.

The instrument consists of seven tactical components that are said to be associated with effective game performance, and these are shown in table 12.1. Depending on the game and game category, a teacher can select one or several of the elements of game play seen in the table to evaluate the performance of individuals in that game.

For the purposes of this book, particularly given that game play itself is secondary to game design, the focus is on the two most used parts of the GPAI—decision making and skill execution.

TABLE 12.1—Components of the GPAI

Game component	Description of the activity
Base	Appropriate return of a performer to a base position between skill attempts
Decision making	Appropriate decisions about what to do with the implement during a game
Skill execution	Efficient execution of the selected skills
Support	Appropriate support for a teammate with the implement by being in position to receive a pass
Guard/mark	Appropriate guarding/marking of an opponent who may or may not have the implement
Cover	Appropriate defensive cover, help, or backup for a player making a challenge for the implement
Adjust	Movement of performer, either offensively or defensively, as necessitated by the game

Based on Griffin, Mitchell, and Oslin, 2006.

The most accurate way for students to score the GPAI is to make tallies for each instance that a player conducts a specific action. The tally options include appropriate/efficient responses (A) or inappropriate/inefficient responses (I). At the end of a game, the amounts of appropriate/efficient and inappropriate/inefficient actions are totaled, and an individual component index can be constructed. The two most common indexes are the decision-making index [DMI = A/(A + IA)] and the skill-execution index [SEI = E/(E + IE)], and as noted, it is these that we will focus on in this chapter. Figure 12.2 provides an example of a score sheet from a game of badminton.

Badminton Scoring Instrument

Player: _____   Coder: _____

Directions:
- Observe your selected player only. Don't worry about the opponent.
- Each time your player makes a shot, make a check in the appropriate box.
- Remember, you will have to make two checks (one for the decision, and one for the outcome).

Game Components

1. Decision making:
   - Appropriate: The striker made a shot that forced the opponent to move away from home or recovery position or one that gave the receiver little time to react to the shuttle (e.g., the striker hit the shuttle really fast and straight at the opponent).
   - Inappropriate: The receiver did not have to move very far to return the shuttle.

2. Skill execution:
   - Efficient: The striker made a shot that would have landed in the opponent's court.
   - Inefficient: The shot went out or didn't clear the net.

PLAYER'S NAME	DECISION MAKING		SKILL EXECUTION	
	Appropriate	Inappropriate	Efficient	Inefficient
Total				

FIGURE 12.2   Sample GPAI sheet for badminton.

In tables 12.2-12.6, there has been an attempt to define the appropriate actions for the five game types as simply but as meaningfully as possible. Certainly, execution is usually easier to quantify with yes or no answers: Did the ball cross the net? Did the batter put the ball into play? Did the player catch the pass? Did the player throw accurately to a receiver? However, as noted, the decision criteria present in these tables are designed to be of somewhat low inference.

TABLE 12.2—Decision and Execution Components for Tag Games

Decisions made	Execution success
By the chaser: Goes after a person very close, is trapped in a corner, or is slow *By the fleer:* Stays at a distance from the chaser or uses dodging or changing of speeds to get away	*For the chaser:* Makes a tag or forces the fleer into a situation where another person could tag *For the fleer:* Is not tagged

TABLE 12.3—Decision and Execution Components for Target Games

Decisions made	Execution success
By the sender: Uses the appropriate club and can explain the purpose of the shot	*For the sender:* Places the object in the target area nominated

TABLE 12.4—Decision and Execution Components for Invasion Games

Decisions made	Execution success
By the player in possession: Takes an open shot, moves with the ball to a better position that allows a shot or pass, passes the ball to a teammate in a better position to score or progress, or maintains control of the ball if none of these are available *By the off-the-ball attacker:* Creates space for herself or for ball carrier *By the on-the-ball defender:* Moves to take away the scoring or progression option of the player in possession *By the off-the-ball defender* Stays between the off-the-ball attacker and target, defends the on-the-ball attacker, defends potential receiver	*For the player in possession:* Scores, moves to a better position, makes a controllable pass, maintains possession *For the off-the-ball attacker:* Creates a passing pathway, creates a shield for ball carrier *For the on-the-ball defender:* Gets the ball or stops ball carrier from achieving outcomes *For the off-the-ball defender:* Defends player or zone, shows awareness of ball carrier

TABLE 12.5—Decision and Execution Components for Striking and Fielding Games

Decisions made	Execution success
By the pitcher/bowler: Bowls to cause desired execution: (1) with speed, (2) with swing/spin, (3) to field (i.e., right or left), or (4) to batter's weakness *By the striker:* Hits to achieve desired outcome: (1) protect target, (2) make an opponent run, or (3) create an opportunity to score *By the fielder:* (1) attacks to prevent score or to force out or (2) defends to prevent further score	*For the pitcher/bowler:* Hits the target or denies a score *For the striker:* Protects the bowling target or forces the opponent to move *For the fielder:* Causes an out or prevents a score

TABLE 12.6—Decision and Execution Components for Net and Wall Games

Decisions made	Execution success
By the striker: Makes a shot that forces the opponent away from home or recovery position or one that gives the opponent little time to react to the oncoming object	*For the striker:* Makes a shot that would have landed in the opponent's court

Evaluating Games

You will recall from previous chapters that we define a good game as one that is fun, fair, and safe. The rubric outlined in assessment 12.4 (page 171) has been developed and refined over a series of games-making units with the goal of capturing the elements of games that contribute to their enjoyment and success. In addition, a further goal was to make the scale easy to use by students for quick referencing of where they believed there were shortfalls in other students' games.

Before completing the scale, students are introduced to the game by the group that designed it. Everyone will then play for a designated period of time following which they will complete the rubric. Given that two teams will usually play, the team that designed the game will receive two sets of feedback. The teacher may also wish to complete an evaluation as well.

The scale uses the technique known as a semantic differential, in which the players are asked to indicate their position on a scale between two bipolar adjective pairs (e.g., boring and exciting). Players simply place a check mark in the appropriate box. If a specific score is required, just add the points values for each item. Those on the far left are considered the least desirable and score 1, while those on the right are the more desired and score 7.

The scoring rubric shown in assessment 12.5 (page 172) is one that should be suitable for younger and less experienced games makers. It still provides feedback about the key elements of good games but limits these to the essential components of enjoyment, understanding, opportunity to play, and fairness. Players simply place a circle around the number that best matches their thoughts about a particular component of the game.

Although some younger students might struggle to come up with new ideas when creating their games, many older students begin a search for innovation and creativity early on in the design process. The rating scale in assessment 12.6 (page 173) can be used in the early stages of game design and focuses on a game's novelty. Its aim is to give feedback to games designers about how creative they have been in choosing their initial rules. In this rating scale, the players comment upon four key areas of game play: (1) scoring system, (2) equipment, (3) playing area, and (4) player limitations (e.g., are there specific zones in which only certain players may be?).

Conclusion

Although many consider assessment to be a mechanism for testing and awarding grades, assessment in the games-making process should be seen as motivating and continuous. This chapter presents a number of instruments that can be used for self- and peer assessment in order to help students learn more about how games work and, ultimately, to help them design good games: games that are *fun, fair, and safe* for all participants.

References

Bocchino, R. (1999). *Emotional literacy: To be a different kind of smart.* Thousand Oaks, CA: Corwin Press.

Grehaigne, J.F., Richard, J.F., & Griffin, L. (2005). *Teaching and learning team sports and games.* New York: RoutledgeFalmer.

Griffin, L.L., Mitchell, S.A., & Oslin, J.L. (2006). *Teaching sport concepts and skills: A tactical games approach.* (2nd ed.). Champaign, IL: Human Kinetics.

Melograno, V.J. (1997). Integrating assessment into physical education teaching. *Journal of Physical Education, Recreation and Dance, 68* (7), 34-37.

Oslin, J.L., Mitchell, S.A., & Griffin, L.L. (1998). The Game Performance Assessment Instrument (GPAI): Development and preliminary validation. *Journal of Teaching in Physical Education, 17,* 231-243.

Approach Tendencies

Student: _____

Observe the student on three different occasions. For each desired behavior, indicate Yes, Sometimes, or No in the appropriate column.

Desired behavior	First observation	Second observation	Third observation
Seeks opportunities to learn			
Practices hard			
Accepts advice			
Participates with enthusiasm			

Personal and Social Responsibility

Student: _____

This assessment can be completed by students as a self-assessment or peer assessment, or by the teacher. First, circle the appropriate recorder in the top row. Second, for each desired attitude, indicate Yes, Sometimes, or No in the appropriate column.

Desired attitude	Self	Peer	Teacher
Takes responsibility for designated role			
Cooperates with others			
Is tolerant toward others			
Shows a commitment to the team			
Plays fairly			

ASSESSMENT 12.3

Knowledge

• •

Student: _____

For each desired skill, check the appropriate column to indicate the student's observed level.

Desired skill	Novice	Emerging	Mastery
Analysis of selected game-strategy problems			
Ability to develop solutions to game problems			
Explanation of student's own game			
Competence in officiating and keeping score			

Game Play Evaluation

Student: _____

Place a check in the box that matches your feelings about the game you have just played. The boxes toward the middle represent a neutral opinion, while those closer to the edges represent a stronger opinion either way.

Boring	☐ ☐ ☐ ☐ ☐ ☐ ☐	Exciting
Low activity	☐ ☐ ☐ ☐ ☐ ☐ ☐	High activity
Too simple	☐ ☐ ☐ ☐ ☐ ☐ ☐	Provoked strategy
Too complicated	☐ ☐ ☐ ☐ ☐ ☐ ☐	Easy to understand
Too much waiting	☐ ☐ ☐ ☐ ☐ ☐ ☐	Everyone involved
Bad player number	☐ ☐ ☐ ☐ ☐ ☐ ☐	Playing number right
No skill developed	☐ ☐ ☐ ☐ ☐ ☐ ☐	Developed skills well
Bad explanation	☐ ☐ ☐ ☐ ☐ ☐ ☐	Excellent explanation
Poor refereeing	☐ ☐ ☐ ☐ ☐ ☐ ☐	Excellent refereeing
Scoring too complex	☐ ☐ ☐ ☐ ☐ ☐ ☐	Good scoring system
Wrong playing area	☐ ☐ ☐ ☐ ☐ ☐ ☐	Good playing area
Wrong equipment	☐ ☐ ☐ ☐ ☐ ☐ ☐	Good equipment
Poor safety	☐ ☐ ☐ ☐ ☐ ☐ ☐	Safety addressed

ASSESSMENT 12.5

Simplified Game Play Evaluation

Student: _____

Circle a number from 1 (not very much) to 10 (a lot) for each of the five questions about the game you have just played.

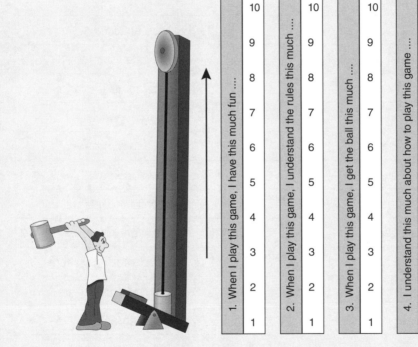

1. When I play this game, I have this much fun ....
   10 9 8 7 6 5 4 3 2 1

2. When I play this game, I understand the rules this much ....
   10 9 8 7 6 5 4 3 2 1

3. When I play this game, I get the ball this much ....
   10 9 8 7 6 5 4 3 2 1

4. I understand this much about how to play this game ....
   10 9 8 7 6 5 4 3 2 1

5. When I play this game, I think it is this fair ....
   10 9 8 7 6 5 4 3 2 1

ASSESSMENT 12.6

Game Creativity Evaluation

Student: _____

For each of the four components of the game you have just played, place a check in the box that matches your feelings about that aspect.

	Seen it, done it	Nothing really new	New but unworkable	New and interesting	Never seen it, want to do it
Scoring system					
Equipment					
Playing area					
Player limitations					

From P. Hastie, 2010, *Student-Designed Games: Strategies for Promoting Creativity, Cooperation, and Skill Development* (Champaign, IL: Human Kinetics).

Index

Note: The letters *f* and *t* after page numbers indicate figures and tables, respectively.

About the Author

Peter Hastie, professor in the department of kinesiology at Auburn University, has been teaching strategies for student designed games in both schools and universities. He has also researched the potential of student designed games to help students become more engaged in physical education, as well as develop a deeper understanding of games. Dr. Hastie is a member of AAHPERD, American Educational Research Association (AERA), and International Association for Physical Education in Higher Education (AIESEP). He enjoys whitewater rafting, traveling, and overland trekking.

You'll find other outstanding physical education resources at
www.HumanKinetics.com

In the U.S. call 1.800.747.4457
Australia 08 8372 0999
Canada. 1.800.465.7301
Europe . . . . .+44 (0) 113 255 5665
New Zealand 0800 222 062

HUMAN KINETICS
The Information Leader in Physical Activity & Health
P.O. Box 5076 • Champaign, IL 61825-5076